A Photographic Geography of Alaska

ALASKA GEOGRAPHIC®
Volume 7, Number 2, 1980
Revised 1983

The Alaska Geographic Society

To teach many more to better know and use our natural resources

Editors: Robert A. Henning, Barbara Olds, Penny Rennick
Associate Editors: Margy Kotick, Lael Morgan, Carol Phillips
Designer: Dianne Hofbeck
Cartographer: Jon.Hersh
Illustrator: Val Paul Taylor

Editor's note: Population figures for this issue are based on the 1980 Census of Population, U.S. Department of Commerce, Bureau of the Census; and the 1981 Alaska Population Overview, Alaska Department of Labor.

Copyright ©1980, 1983 by
The Alaska Geographic Society
All rights reserved.
Registered Trademark: *Alaska Geographic.*
ISSN 0361-1353; key title *Alaska Geographic.*
ISBN 0-88240-173-4

ALASKA GEOGRAPHIC®, ISSN 0361-1353, is published quarterly by The Alaska Geographic Society, Anchorage, Alaska 99509. Second-class postage paid in Edmonds, Washington 98020. Printed in U.S.A.

THE ALASKA GEOGRAPHIC SOCIETY is a non-profit organization exploring new frontiers of knowledge across the lands of the polar rim, learning how other men and other countries live in their Norths, putting the geography book back in the classroom, exploring new methods of teaching and learning — sharing in the excitement of discovery in man's wonderful new world north of 51°16′.

MEMBERS OF THE SOCIETY RECEIVE *Alaska Geographic®*, a quality magazine in color which devotes each quarterly issue to monographic in-depth coverage of a northern geographic region or resource-oriented subject.

MEMBERSHIP DUES in The Alaska Geographic Society are $30 per year; $34 to non-U.S. addresses, U.S. funds. (Eighty percent of each year's dues is for a one-year subscription to *Alaska Geographic®*.)

Order from The Alaska Geographic Society, Box 4-EEE, Anchorage, Alaska 99509; (907) 274-0521.

MATERIAL SOUGHT: The editors of *Alaska Geographic®* seek a wide variety of informative material on the lands north of 51°16′ on geographic subjects— anything to do with resources and their uses (with heavy emphasis on quality color photography)—from Alaska, Northern Canada, Siberia, Japan—all geographic areas that have a relationship to Alaska in a physical or economic sense. We do not want material done in excessive scientific terminology. A query to the editors is suggested. Payments are made for all material upon publication.

CHANGE OF ADDRESS: The post office does not automatically forward *Alaska Geographic®* when you move. To ensure continuous service, notify us six weeks before moving. Send us your new address and zip code (and moving date), your old address and zip code, and if possible send a mailing label from a copy of *Alaska Geographic®*. Send this information to *Alaska Geographic®* Mailing Offices, 130 Second Avenue South, Edmonds, Washington 98020.

MAILING LISTS: We have begun making our members' names and addresses available to carefully screened publications and companies whose products and activities might be of interest to you. If you would prefer not to receive such mailings, please so advise us, and include your mailing label (or your name and address if label is not available).

The cover: The six Alaskas within Alaska.
►Top row from left, Auke Bay near Juneau in Southeast; see chapter beginning on page 8. (The Jerrold Olsons) / Wonder Lake, Denali National Park in the Interior; see page 54. (Jim Shives) / Columbia Glacier, Prince William Sound, in the Southcentral/Gulf Coast region; see page 30. (Ron Dalby)
►Bottom row from left, polar bear on an ice floe in the Arctic; see page 110. (Steve McCutcheon) / Banding geese on Buldir Island in the Aleutians; see page 74. (R.H. Day) / Leads in the pack ice along the Bering Sea coast; see page 92. (Steve Leatherwood)

Contents page
Russell Glacier on Chitistone Pass separates the Wrangell from the Saint Elias mountains. The shoulder of 16,421-foot Mount Bona is on the left horizon; peaks of the University Range are on center and right horizon.
(George Herben)

Below
Old Rampart, on the right bank of the Porcupine River, was once one of the largest settlements on the river.
(Alan C. Paulson)

Introduction

Alaska is so vast, so thinly populated, and has so many insular villages and cities separated one from the other by great distances that it is difficult to visualize, even for local residents. Most residents know little about most of Alaska . . . and that just about sums up the situation. There is a growing library of published Alaska material, from the seen-by-few Aleutian Islands to the heavily populated Rail Belt, the Anchorage and Fairbanks area, to the disconnected "panhandle" of southeastern Alaska and its glaciers and fjords as well as the bleak but oil-rich arctic slope in the opposite direction . . . but unfortunately much of it is either stuffy academic material or rehash of older and also thin research resulting too often in the "quickie" book or article by another two-week visitor. As we've said, the Alaskan resident himself often knows but little about this big country. Even we in The Alaska Geographic Society and Alaska Northwest Publishing, whose business has been digging for Alaska knowledge and publishing for nearly half a century, must admit we are constantly discovering new elements of Alaska, even newly explored physical areas. So don't feel badly if you regret your knowledge of Alaska is limited. So is ours.

Because the job of "doing an Alaska geography" is so big, so complex, we felt this compendium of a lot of wonderful color photos and a digest of "adequate" information . . . facts . . . would serve better to impart an improved understanding of Alaska in all its aspects. We've borrowed heavily from *ALASKA*® magazine, from other issues of *ALASKA GEOGRAPHIC*® and from our *ALASKA ALMANAC*. We hope you enjoy it. In a sense it is our family album.

—The Editors

Separated by the waters of Iliuliuk Harbor, Unalaska (foreground) and Dutch Harbor on adjacent Amaknak Island are one community for business purposes.
(Ben Kirker)

The Six Alaskas

Aleutia

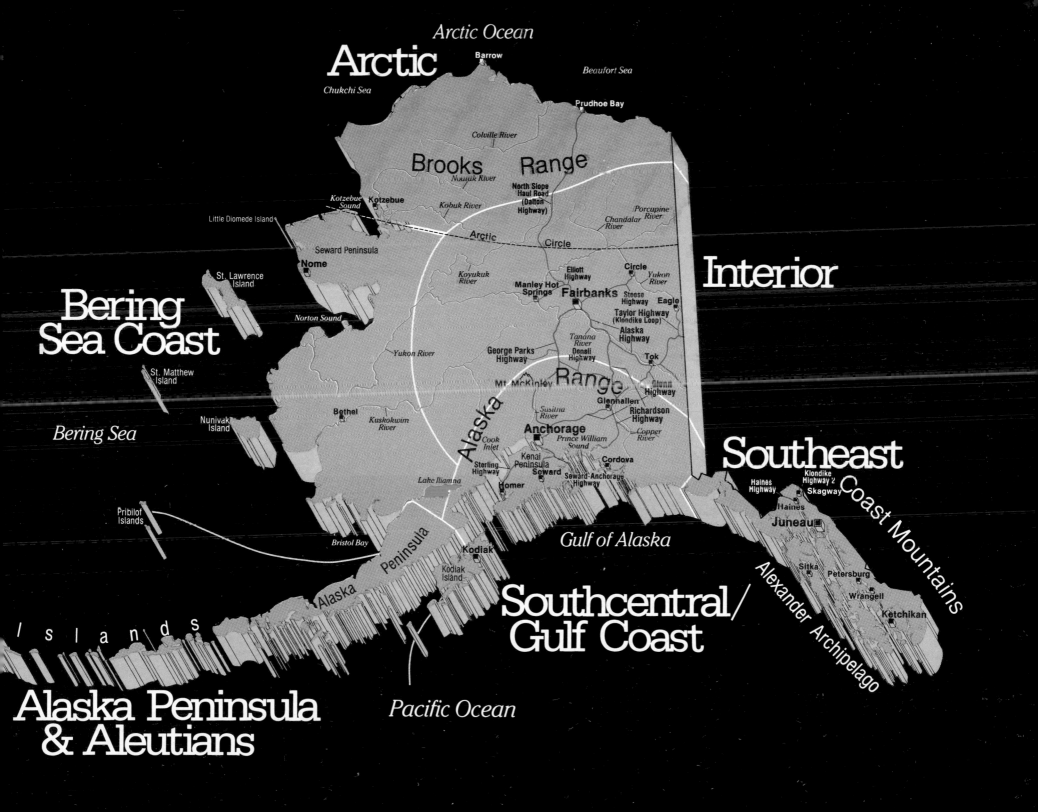

Arctic

Arctic Ocean

Barrow

Chukchi Sea

Beaufort Sea

Prudhoe Bay

Colville River

Brooks Range

Nouluk River

North Slope Haul Road (Dalton Highway)

Porcupine River

Kotzebue Sound

Kotzebue

Kobuk River

Chandalar River

Little Diomede Island

Arctic Circle

Seward Peninsula

Interior

Nome

Koyukuk River

Elliott Highway

Circle

Yukon River

Bering Sea Coast

St. Lawrence Island

Manley Hot Springs

Fairbanks

Steese Highway

Eagle

Taylor Highway (Klondike Loop)

Norton Sound

Yukon River

George Parks Highway

Tanana River

Alaska Highway

St. Matthew Island

Denali Highway

Tok

Mt. McKinley

Alaska Range

Glenn Highway

Bering Sea

Susitna River

Glennallen

Richardson Highway

Bethel

Kuskokwim River

Anchorage

Prince William Sound

Copper River

Nunivak Island

Cook Inlet

Kenai Peninsula

Cordova

Southeast

Sterling Highway

Seward

Lake Iliamna

Homer

Seward-Anchorage Highway

Haines Highway

Klondike Highway 2

Skagway

Pribilof Islands

Haines

Juneau

Bristol Bay

Kodiak

Gulf of Alaska

Sitka

Petersburg

Peninsula

Kodiak Island

Southcentral/ Gulf Coast

Wrangell

Ketchikan

Alexander Archipelago

Coast Mountains

I s l a n d s

Alaska

Alaska Peninsula & Aleutians

Pacific Ocean

Southeast

Forested islands and glacier-scoured fjords against a mountain backdrop... this is Southeast, the panhandle that extends some 560 miles from Dixon Entrance near Ketchikan to Icy Bay north of Yakutat. Geological activity has sculpted more than a thousand islands in Southeast, including Prince of Wales, third largest in the United States at 2,231 square miles. The region's narrow strip of mainland is isolated from the rest of North America by the Saint Elias and Coast mountain ranges. Mount Saint Elias (18,008 feet), Mount Vancouver (15,700 feet), Mount Fairweather (15,300 feet) and other lofty peaks make the Saint Elias the highest coastal range in the world.

Average precipitation in Southeast is more than 100 inches in many spots, ranging from 26 inches at Skagway to 227 inches at Little Port Walter on Baranof Island. Warm ocean currents moderate the region's climate. Summer temperatures average close to 60°F. Sub-zero temperatures are not common in winter and the thermometer usually hovers in the mid-thirties. At lower elevations snows often melt within a few days; higher up, more than 200 inches are recorded each year—snow that continually feeds the 40-by-100-mile Juneau Icefield.

Heavy rainfall and a mild climate encourage timber growth and more than 73 percent of Southeast is covered with dense forests. Covering 16 million acres, the Tongass National Forest, composed primarily of western hemlock and Sitka spruce interspersed with red cedar and Alaska yellow cedar, is the nation's largest. Ground cover is lush and includes devil's club, blueberries, huckleberries, mosses and ferns.

The heavy timber and dense undergrowth is prime habitat for Sitka blacktail deer, wolves and bears. Brown/grizzlies inhabit Admiralty, Baranof and Chichagof islands (no wolves) and the mainland; black bears inhabit other forested islands and the mainland. Mountain goats, lynx, wolverines, foxes, mink, river otters, porcupines, marten, scattered populations of moose,

available to virtually any spot in Southeast. Because the islands and mountainous terrain of Southeast make highway construction between communities impossible, a fleet of Alaska state ferries move people and vehicles between this region's communities, and also connect the panhandle with Seattle, Washington, and Prince Rupert, British Columbia (at the end of Yellowhead Highway 16). Only two southeastern communities are connected to the Alaska Highway system: Haines, via the Haines Highway; and Skagway, via Klondike Highway 2.

Ketchikan, with an area population of 11,373, serves as the southern gateway to the region. For many years the huge salmon catches for which Southeast was famous centered around this port. Today the pulp and timber industry, tourism, fishing and the related business of fish processing and cold storage support the economy.

Timber forms the basis for the major industry for Ketchikan and most of Southeast. Ketchikan Spruce Mill, now part of Louisiana Pacific, Ketchikan Division, was founded in 1903 and is the longest continuously operated mill in the state. Louisiana Pacific also operates a pulp mill just north of Ketchikan. The sawmill's capacity is about 400,000 board feet per shift, with production depending on the quality of logs and market conditions; the pulp is rated at 600 tons per day. The pulp, a dissolving variety suitable for breads, frostings, pharmaceuticals, photo film, rayon and cellophane, is shipped to domestic and foreign markets. Outlying camps supply logs for Louisiana Pacific's operations in the Ketchikan area.

Several communities near Ketchikan rely on fishing or logging for their livelihood. Metlakatla, in addition to being the site of the Annette Island sawmill, has had a salmon cannery since 1890. Hyder, tucked away at the end of 70-mile-long Portland Canal, is a former mining boom town. A side road off the Cassiar Highway connects Hyder with its neighbor, Stewart, British Columbia, and the rest of the continent. Meyers Chuck, north of Ketchikan on

Above
One of the many access routes to Alaska is the Inside Passage, a water route from Seattle, Washington, to Skagway, Alaska. This ferry is passing through Grenville Channel, south of Prince Rupert, British Columbia.
(Sally Bishop)

Opposite
Devils Thumb (9,077 feet) rises on the Alaska-Canada border northeast of Petersburg.
(Michio Hoshino)

and an assortment of small mammals range throughout Southeast. The region boasts the largest bald eagle population in the world.

Three-fourths of Southeast's 56,000 residents live in five major urban areas: Ketchikan, Wrangell, Petersbug, Sitka and Juneau. About 25 smaller communities, some with fewer than 50 inhabitants, are scattered among the islands and mainland. Tlingit, Haida and Tsimshian Indians live in the major communities and in traditional villages such as Klukwan, Hoonah, Angoon, Kasaan, Kake, Klawock, Hydaburg and Metlakatla.

Access to southeastern Alaska is by air or by ferry. Scheduled air service and charter air service is

the Cleveland Peninsula, is a small fishing village that was dying a few years ago but has lately seen an increase in activity.

About 45 miles east of Ketchikan is one of the largest deposits of molybdenum sulfide in the world. Discovered in 1974 by U.S. Borax and Chemical Corporation, development of the site was delayed by environmental concerns (the deposit lies within Misty Fiords National Monument) and the rugged terrain. U.S. Borax was finally granted permission to take bulk samples from the deposit to determine its value, and construction of a temporary access road began in 1982. The United States is the world's major producer of molybdenum, a mineral used as a steel alloy to increase durability, lighten weight and provide thermal flexibility.

Several towns dependent on fishing and/or logging are nestled on Prince of Wales Island. Ferries stop at Hollis on the east side of the island and from there you can travel by road to Craig, Klawock and Thorne Bay. Mining, especially for copper, has always been important to this region, and while none of the mining camps have survived, there is still much prospecting activity in the area.

About 85 miles northwest of Ketchikan is Wrangell, population about 2,350, the only Alaska city to have existed under three flags—Russian, British and American. Wrangell began in 1834 as a Russian stockade called Redoubt Saint Dionysius. In 1840, the British took over the post and renamed it Fort Stikine. The United States purchased Alaska from Russia in 1867 and a year later established Fort Wrangell. Wrangell's location near the mouth of the Stikine River made the town an important supply point for fur traders and also for gold seekers. Prospectors came through Wrangell bound for the Stikine gold strike in 1861, for the Cassiar in 1874, and for the Klondike gold fields in 1898. Mainstays of the community's economy today are lumber and fishing. Alaska Lumber and Pulp Company has a milling operation here which processes primarily spruce. Salmon is the major fish catch; halibut, herring, and shrimp are also caught and processed in Wrangell.

Midway between Ketchikan and Juneau is Petersburg, population about 3,000. Spread out along the shores of Mitkof Island, Petersburg thrives on a modern fishing industry. The first cannery was built in 1900 by Peter Buschmann. Known today as Petersburg Fisheries, a division of Icicle Seafoods, this most advanced fish plant processes canned salmon, herring, herring roe, king crab, tanner crab, salmon eggs, and halibut. Fish meal is produced from recycled wastes. Other seafood plants in Petersburg are Alaskan Glacier Seafood, oldest shrimp cannery in Alaska; Whitney-Fidalgo Seafoods; and Nelbro Packing Company. In the midst of all the fish processing is Mitkof Lumber, a small mill that handles local spruce and hemlock.

Sitka, population 7,927, is located on the west coast of Baranof Island at the foot of Harbor Mountain and looks out over an archipelago of islands to the vast North Pacific. Once the capital of Russian America, Sitka is capitalizing on its rich historical past and scenic appeal and tourism is becoming a leading factor in the town's economy. Other major economic forces include the Japanese-owned Alaska Lumber and Pulp Mill, commercial fishing and fish processing, as well as the federal government—the Coast Guard, Forest Service, Alaska Native Health Service, Bureau of Indian Affairs and Sheldon Jackson College.

Government is the economic foundation of the state capital, Juneau, with more than 20,000 residents. An estimated 25 percent of the city's workers are employed in various branches of borough, state and federal government. Three smaller suburbs— Douglas, across Gastineau Channel on Douglas Island, and Mendenhall Valley and Auke Bay north of Juneau—have prospered from the commercial and government activity of Juneau. Mendenhall Glacier, a major tourist attraction and the only glacier in Southeast accessible by road, deposits icebergs into Mendenhall Lake about 12 miles north of town.

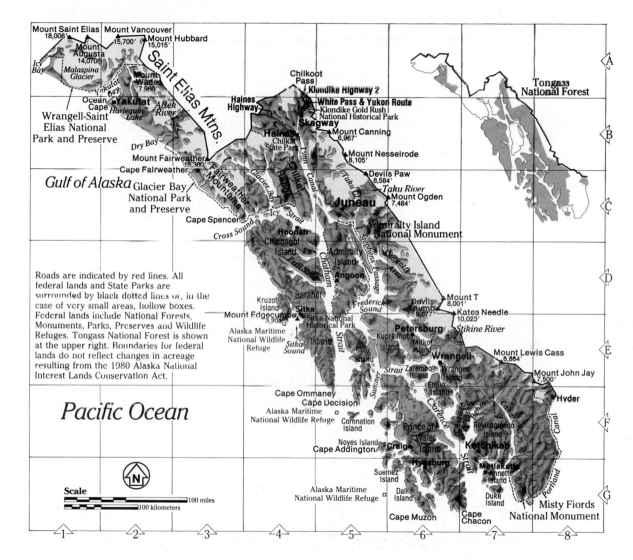

Discovery of gold in 1880 led to the founding of Juneau. Today the legendary early mines are silent; but rising metal prices have generated a resurgence of mining activity. As in all towns in Southeast, fishing plays an important role in the economy.

Northwest of Juneau lies Glacier Bay, where icebergs calve from 16 active tidewater glaciers and spread throughout myriad bays and inlets of the 3.3-million-acre Glacier Bay National Park and Preserve. The small community of Gustavus, nearest to the park, is connected by a nine-mile road from the airport to park headquarters at Bartlett Cove.

The park's icy waterways are a regular summer feeding area for humpback whales. (Research indicates some of these same whales winter in the waters off the Hawaiian Islands.) Humpbacks are easily identified by their huge flippers.

East of Glacier Bay is 60-mile-long Lynn Canal, the passage between the Coast Mountains and the Chilkat Range that provides water access to Haines, on Chilkoot Inlet, and Skagway, near the head of Taiya Inlet.

Originally founded as a Presbyterian mission in 1881, Haines was a mining supply center for various gold rushes until the mid-1920s, as well as a fishing port and salmon canning center. In the early 1900s the U.S. government built a permanent military base at nearby Port Chilkoot overlooking Portage Cove. In 1970 Haines and Port Chilkoot merged. Today, with a population of about 1,070, Haines is the headquarters of a Native cultural center and home port for an active gill-net fleet.

Southeastern Alaska accounts for only a small percentage of the state's agricultural production, but Haines is remembered for its strawberries. Developed by Charles Anway, the Alaskan hybrid was a winner at the 1909 exposition in Seattle.

Leaning dead alders, standing spruce
and some of the lush vegetation at Bartlett Cove
in Glacier Bay National Park and Preserve.
(Michio Hoshino)

Fourteen miles north of Haines by water is Skagway, northern terminus of the Inside Passage and southern terminus of Klondike Highway 2. Skagway was a disembarking point for gold miners bound for the Klondike in 1897-98. Many of the town's old wooden buildings are included in Klondike Gold Rush National Historical Park. Just outside town is the trail head of the Chilkoot Trail, once a major gold rush route to the Klondike, now a historic back-country trail. Paralleling the trail is the White Pass & Yukon Route railroad. Completed in 1900, the rail-road was the only link between Skagway and White-horse until 1978, when the highway was completed.

The northern neck of southeastern Alaska, a narrow coastal stretch from Glacier Bay to Malaspina Glacier, is characterized by mountains, glaciers and generally rugged terrain. There are few harbors and even fewer signs of human activity between Glacier Bay and Yakutat Bay.

Yakutat, with its harbor on Monti Bay and huge Yakutat Bay just beyond some nearshore islands, is the only community in the area. Fishing supports this mostly Tlingit community of 430. Across the bay to the north lies the ice mass of Malaspina Glacier, largest in North America. The skyline is dominated by Mount Saint Elias, 18,008 feet, and in the far distance by Canada's Mount Logan, at 19,850 feet the second-highest peak on the continent.

A humpback whale diving in Stephens Passage, an 80-mile-long channel from Portland Island to Frederick Sound, south of Juneau.
(Lou Barr, reprinted from *ALASKA GEOGRAPHIC*®)

15

Below
Ketchikan, population about 11,300, is the first major Alaska community encountered by visitors coming up the Inside Passage from Seattle, hence Ketchikan's nickname, First City.
(Matthew Donohoe)

Left
Some early-day buildings still stand in downtown Wrangell despite two serious fires in this century. Today Wrangell, population about 2,350, thrives on fishing, lumber and tourism.
(Staff, reprinted from *ALASKA GEOGRAPHIC*®)

Below
Aerial photograph of Petersburg, at the north end of the Wrangell Narrows. The community, known as Alaska's "Little Norway," is a fishing center.
(Dick Estelle)

Above

At Shakes Island in Wrangell are some of the oldest Tlingit houseposts. The posts (above right) were carved before 1800 and were moved from the Tlingit village of Kotslitan (Old Wrangell) to Shakes Island in 1869.
(Both photos by Barry Herem, reprinted from *ALASKA*® magazine)

Right

The braided channel of the Stikine River close to its mouth near Wrangell. The river rises in northern British Columbia and flows 400 miles to the sea.
(Staff, reprinted from *ALASKA*® magazine)

Left
John Bobner cuts a Sitka spruce log, a valuable timber species in Southeast.
(Steve McCutcheon)

Below
The freighter, Atlantic Pioneer, waits at the dock in Metlakatla, on Annette Island. This Tsimshian Indian community's economy is based on logging, sawmilling, fish harvesting and fish processing. It is the only community in Alaska that is organized under federal law.
(S. Forrest Blau)

Right
Piles of wood chips for processing into pulp at the Ketchikan mill.
(Matthew Donohoe)

18

Left
Beautiful Sitka, as seen from Harbor Mountain. This community of about 7,900 was once the capital of Russian America and is now a center for fishing, timber and pulp processing, education and tourism.
(Ed Cooper)

Below
The spires and domes of Saint Michael's Cathedral in Sitka. The original structure, which was built in 1844-48, burned in 1966. The doors and many of the icons were saved and the church was rebuilt.
(Mark Kelley)

Left
Juneau, the state capital, spreads out on the mainland on the far side of 19-mile-long Gastineau Channel. The community of Douglas, on Douglas Island, is in the foreground.
(William Bacon III)

Below
Mendenhall Glacier and Lake viewed from the visitor center, 13 miles north of Juneau. Named for Professor Thomas Corwin Mendenhall, a superintendent of the U.S. Coast and Geodetic Survey, the glacier is accessible by road and is a major scenic attraction.
(John Helle, reprinted from *ALASKA GEOGRAPHIC®*)

Above
Cruise ships and a small plane that flies sightseers over the Juneau Icefield lie at rest at the Juneau harbor.
(Mark M. Smith)

Right
The Governor's Mansion in Juneau, completed in 1913, was built and furnished for $40,000.
(Ed Cooper)

21

Left
For years life for many southeasterners revolved around fishing. Ketchikan billed itself as the salmon capital of the world. While not as important as it used to be, fishing is still a major economic force in Southeast. This fisherman is preparing to gaff a king salmon.
(Matthew Donohoe)

Lower left
Fishermen work a trap at Metlakatla, on Annette Island. Only Natives are allowed to operate traps.
(Kirk Mathews)

Below
Old rooming houses and other buildings line the shore of Port Alexander, a fishing community near the southern tip of Baranof Island.
(Charlie Ott)

Left
The first salmon cannery in Alaska opened in Klawock in 1878 and the village has maintained its ties with the fishing industry ever since. Today about 390 residents, primarily Tlingits, live in this community on the west side of Prince of Wales Island.
(Stephen Hilson, reprinted from *ALASKA GEOGRAPHIC®*)

Below
The serene waters of Elfin Cove, near the north tip of Chichagof Island, reflect the fishing boats and buildings of the small community with the same name on the east shore of the cove.
(Jim Nilsen)

Left
Both black and brown/grizzly bears inhabit Southeast. This black bear was photographed near the North Arm of Dundas Bay in Glacier Bay National Park and Preserve.
(William Boehm)

Below
Sitka blacktail deer swim across a narrow channel in Olga Strait, near Sitka.
(Harold Wahlman, reprinted from *Alaska: A Pictorial Geography*)

Right
The fishing community of Angoon, the majority of whose 465 inhabitants are Tlingit Indians, is the only permanent settlement on Admiralty Island in central Southeast.
(Stephen Hilson, reprinted from *ALASKA GEOGRAPHIC®*)

Right
Historic Skagway, at the north end of Taiya Inlet on Lynn Canal, is the oldest incorporated city in Alaska and a year-round port. Skagway owes its beginning to the Klondike gold rush when miners seeking their fortune in the gold fields near Dawson City, Yukon Territory, disembarked at Skagway and Dyea before heading over Chilkoot Pass and White Pass. A six-block district in the heart of Skagway has been designated as a portion of the Klondike Gold Rush National Historical Park, which commemorates the great stampede.
(George Wuerthner)

Left
Originally known as Fort William H. Seward, Chilkoot Barracks, as it became known in the 1920s, was one of five early military posts built in Alaska. The barracks were maintained until the 1940s. Several years ago the site was purchased by a World War II veterans group that became interested in preserving Native culture. In 1972 Chilkoot Barracks was designated a national historic site and again became officially known as Fort William H. Seward.
(George Wuerthner)

Right
Bergs from Muir Glacier drift out Muir Inlet in Glacier Bay National Park and Preserve on their way to the sea.
(Michio Hoshino)

Left
A section of Hubbard Glacier calves into Disenchantment Bay east of Yakutat. Scientists are studying the movement of the glacier, named for Gardiner G. Hubbard, the first president of the National Geographic Society, to see if a forward thrust of the glacier might cut off Russell Fiord from Disenchantment Bay.
(Steve McCutcheon)

Right
The isolated Pacific coast south of Yakutat. Few people visit this area of Alaska where the lush coastal vegetation backs against the glaciers of the Saint Elias and Fairweather mountains.
(Bill Harrigan)

Southcentral/ Gulf Coast

Southcentral/Gulf Coast has come of the most rugged terrain in Alaska and the state's biggest population center. Sandwiched between lofty peaks of the Alaska Range and the Gulf of Alaska, the region ranges west from the Yakutat area to include Kodiak Island, the Kenai Peninsula and Cook Inlet.

Southcentral's mainland is a roller coaster topography of high mountains and broad river valleys. To the east the Copper, Chitina and Matanuska rivers are hemmed in by the Chugach, Wrangell and Talkeetna mountains and the crest of the Alaska Range. To the west the Susitna River flows into the muddy upper reaches of Cook Inlet, a 220-mile-long body of water between the Kenai Mountains and Aleutian Range. The other major indentation in the mainland is Prince William Sound, a 15,000-square-mile maze of water, ice and islands. The Kodiak Archipelago extends southwest from the Kenai Peninsula and shields the western flank of the mainland, to some extent, from Gulf of Alaska storms. Kodiak Island, at 3,588 square miles, ranks as the state's largest island.

The climate is maritime—rain and fog—with mild temperature fluctuations. Nearer the mountains, the climate becomes transitional and temperature changes are greater and the climate is generally harsher. In Anchorage, January temperatures average 13° F; July temperatures average 57° F. Protected by the Chugach and Kenai mountains from the moisture-laden clouds from the gulf, Anchorage averages about 15 inches of precipitation annually. However, at Whittier, on the coast, annual average precipitation is 175 inches. Portage, 13 miles away, receives 58 inches a year.

Variable terrain and climate provide suitable habitat for an assortment of plants and wildlife. The moisture-demanding vegetation of Southeast continues along the coast to the Kenai Peninsula and Kodiak. Sitka spruce and western hemlock dominate the coastal forests. Farther inland birch, alder and aspen are the primary species. At higher elevations the forests give way to subalpine brush thickets, fields of wild flowers, berries and alpine meadows. Major river valleys have stands of black cottonwood. Chugach National Forest, created in 1907, encompasses 5.8 million acres of Southcentral's forests.

Variety also characterizes Southcentral's animal populations. Big game species abound. Brown/ grizzly bears, the only large mammal native to Kodiak Island, are equally at home in portions of the Matanuska and Susitna valleys and on the flats on the west side of Cook Inlet. Sitka blacktail deer, mountain goats and Dall sheep have been introduced to Kodiak, and elk to nearby Afognak Island. Mountain goats roam the sheer cliffs of the Chugach and Wrangell mountains. Moose thrive on the Kenai Peninsula, where the nearly 2-million-acre Kenai National Wildlife Refuge provides habitat for the moose and recreation for people. Moose occur throughout the rest of Southcentral, except on islands of Prince William Sound and the Kodiak group. Dall sheep are found in the Talkeetna, Wrangell and Chugach mountains, on the slopes of the Alaska Range and on inland peaks of the Kenai Mountains. Sitka blacktail deer and black and brown/grizzly bears inhabit the coastal forests of Prince William Sound. Wolves reside on the Kenai Peninsula, in the Nelchina basin, the Copper River valley, the Eagle River valley near Anchorage, and in the rolling country northwest of Cook Inlet.

Smaller mammals in the Southcentral/Gulf Coast region include lynx, pine marten, weasels, beaver, muskrat, mink, red foxes, land otters, porcupines, wolverines, snowshoe hares, shrews, voles and lemmings. Southcentral has congregations of bald and golden eagles, hawks and falcons, and an over-whelming number of shorebirds and waterfowl. The

Aerial view of the fishing community of Cordova, population 2,223, with Orca Inlet in the foreground and Eyak Lake in the background.
(Steve McCutcheon)

32

world's population of dusky Canada geese summer on the Copper River flats, and rare trumpeter swans nest on the Kenai Peninsula and near the Copper River.

The rich Gulf Coast waters support shellfish populations of crabs, shrimp and clams. Salmon, herring, cod, Dolly Varden and cutthroat trout abound and nourish, in turn, harbor and Dall porpoise and killer whales. Largest marine mammals in the area are the baleen whales—humpbacks, fins and minkes—which feed on krill and other marine invertebrates that thrive in the nutrient-rich waters.

Anchorage is the center of Alaska's transportation complex. More than a dozen major domestic and foreign air carriers land at Anchorage International, and Lake Hood, just across the road, is one of the largest seaplane bases in the world.

Anchorage began as a railroad construction camp and The Alaska Railroad is still an important carrier of passengers and freight between Anchorage and Fairbanks. Freight routes extend to Seward on the Kenai Peninsula and the railroad operates a spur line from Anchorage to Whittier that transports passengers and vehicles. From Whittier passengers can board the MV *Bartlett,* a state ferry which connects Whittier, Valdez and Cordova. Another ferry, the MV *Tustumena,* serves Seward, Homer, Seldovia, Kodiak, Port Lions, King Cove and Sand Point, as well as Valdez and Cordova.

Cruise ship traffic in Alaska is confined almost entirely to Southeast. Southcentral ports—such as Valdez, Anchorage, Kodiak, and Seward—are busy with containership and tanker traffic.

Alaska is not known for its extensive highway network but of the 15 highways in the state, two major routes—the Glenn and the Seward—pass through Anchorage. The Seward Highway and its offshoot, the Sterling, serve the Kenai Peninsula. The Seward runs south from Anchorage to Seward on Resurrection Bay on the east side of the peninsula (127 miles). The Sterling branches off from the Seward near Kenai Lake and extends west and south for 136 miles to

Homer. The Glenn Highway heads northeast from Anchorage to Glennallen and on to the Alaska Highway (345 miles). About 35 miles out from Anchorage the George Parks Highway meets the Glenn. The Parks, named in honor of territorial governor George Parks, was completed in 1971 and runs 358 miles from Anchorage to Fairbanks past Mount McKinley. The Richardson Highway, the region's other major route, extends north 266 miles from Valdez to Delta Junction on the Alaska Highway. The original road went all the way to Fairbanks but a portion of the Richardson was absorbed by the Alaska Highway with its construction in the 1940s.

At the eastern edge of the Southcentral/Gulf Coast region is 12-million-acre Wrangell-Saint Elias National Park and Preserve.

The coast from Icy Bay to the Copper River Delta is vegetated flatlands pushed seaward by the Robinson Mountains and the large glaciers that flow from the Bagley Icefield in the Chugach Mountains. The coastline offers few refuges from the fury of the Gulf of

Thousands of birds use the Copper River Delta as a breeding ground or a rest stop for flights farther north. The Copper River heads on the north side of the Wrangell Mountains and flows south 250 miles through the Chugach Mountains to the Gulf of Alaska.
(Rose Arvidson)

Alaska and aside from a few families living near Yakataga, the area is relatively uninhabited.

The Copper River, historic gateway to the rich mineral deposits of the Wrangell Mountains, drains into the Gulf of Alaska east of Cordova. The mud flats of the river's delta are a major landfall for migrating shorebirds and waterfowl. Salmon, too, use the river as a route to spawning grounds.

At Hinchinbrook Entrance, the Gulf of Alaska merges with Prince William Sound, home of major salmon fishery, crabbing and shrimping industries. Cordova, population 2,223, is the primary fishing port for the eastern sound. In the 1964 earthquake the townsite rose six to seven feet which left the port facilities high and dry. The Army Corps of Engineers dredged the harbor and built a bulkhead to contain the dredge material. The mud solidified and formed a flat area suitable for new construction. Canneries at Cordova process tanner, king and Dungeness crabs; king, red, coho, chum and pink salmon; razor clams, halibut and herring. The 50-mile Copper River Highway leads east from town past Eyak Lake, and the Sheridan and Sherman glaciers to the Copper River.

West of Cordova on Prince William Sound is Valdez, southern terminus of the 800-mile-long trans-Alaska pipeline. The town had to be rebuilt after the 1964 Good Friday earthquake. The economy of "new" Valdez, population 3,279, is based on support activities for the marine pipeline terminal. (The first tanker load of oil from Prudhoe Bay was shipped out of Valdez in 1977.) The ice-free port of Valdez with its connection to the Richardson Highway is the shortest route to interior Alaska from Lower 48 ports. Shipment of goods along this route stimulates additional revenue as does commercial salmon fishing and tourism.

Columbia Glacier, west of Valdez, is a major visitor attraction. Tour boats and charter flightseeing services from Valdez and Whittier take visitors into Columbia Bay to view the glacier, whose face ranges

INDEX TO SOUTHCENTRAL/GULF COAST GEOGRAPHIC FEATURES

New names established by the 1980 Alaska National Interest Lands Conservation Act are in parentheses following the old name.

Roads are indicated by red lines. All federal lands and State Parks are surrounded by black dotted lines or, in the case of very small areas, hollow boxes. Federal lands include National Forests, Monuments, Parks, Preserves and Wildlife Refuges. Boundaries and names of federal lands do not reflect changes resulting from the 1980 Alaska National Interest Lands Conservation Act. (See index for new names.)

from 164 to 262 feet in height. Harbor seals, bald eagles, black-legged kittiwakes and gulls feed on the rich marine life of the bay.

West of the 440-square-mile mass of Columbia Glacier lies the port of Whittier, population 198, the hub of small boat traffic for western Prince William Sound. Many commercial fishermen operate out of Cordova but when the salmon runs increase in the western sound in late June and July, skippers from Cordova and even from Seward transfer their operations to Whittier.

Thickly forested bays and sheer cliffs characterize the Gulf Coast south and west of Whittier as far as Resurrection Bay and the port of Seward. Fishing, a lumbermill and government-related activities provide jobs for many of the town's residents. Seward's small-boat harbor, modern and well eqiupped, is home port for numerous charter fishing vessels. Sightseeing excursions into Resurrection Bay to offshore islands such as the Chiswells with their large Steller sea lion colonies and thousands of sea birds, and to Aialik Bay, notable for its tidewater glaciers and wildlife, are generating increased tourist dollars. Seward is also a jumping-off point for trips into Kenai Fjords National Park. Flightseeing trips are available over Resurrection Bay and the Harding Icefield.

The southern end of the Kenai Peninsula offers a challenge to adventurers willing to tackle its rugged terrain and sometimes rough coastal waters. Portlock, near the peninsula's tip, was once a small fishing community but the cannery closed and the townsite was abandoned. English Bay, Port Graham and the larger community of Seldovia, population 505, all on the south side of Kachemak Bay, depend on fishing, fish processing and to a lesser extent, lumbering and tourism.

The Sterling Highway ends on the north shore of Kachemak Bay at the fishing and tourist community of Homer. Prospector Homer Pennock earned his place in history by giving his name to a site near the end of four-and-a-half-mile-long Homer Spit where the town and first post office were located. The com-

mercial center of Homer has moved back from the spit over the years and the main downtown streets now extend out from a core area on a bluff above Kachemak Bay.

A comparatively mild climate and relatively quiet living have attracted artists and craftspeople who live side by side with fishermen, businessmen and tradesmen. Processing shrimp, crab, halibut and salmon in season keep the canneries busy. Sport fishing for halibut is also a big industry in Homer, where dozens of charter boats offer their services to visiting fishermen. Rich deposits of coal—collected for home use by some local residents—lie just to the north of Homer.

North of Homer along the Sterling Highway are several small beach-front communities clustered around a cannery or harbor. Cook Inlet beaches are popular with visitors from Anchorage because the clam digging and fishing are great.

Kenai, neighboring North Kenai and Nikiski, comprise the industrial heart of the Kenai Peninsula. Kenai, population 4,558, is the largest town on the peninsula. Oil and gas turn the economic wheels of this community. Some 14 offshore rigs operate in upper Cook Inlet. Pipelines carry oil and gas to onshore plants and loading docks. Industrial giants such as Union Oil Company and Chevron USA operate oil refineries and produce products such as ammonia and urea used for fertilizer. Phillips Petroleum operates a natural gas liquefaction plant, shipping the liquefied natural gas to Japan. The remainder of the Kenai Peninsula's economic base is made up of tourism and salmon fishing and processing.

The Kenai Peninsula is home to about 26,520 people, with Homer, Kenai, Seward, and Soldotna accounting for almost 45 percent of the population. The remainder live in small communities such as Moose Pass (population 76), Hope (population 103), and Anchor Point (population 226).

Near Portage at the head of Turnagain Arm the narrow neck of the peninsula joins the southcentral mainland. Portage Glacier, at the end of a short spur

College Fiord, an estuary in Prince William Sound about 63 miles east of Anchorage, extends 18 miles northeast off Port Wells. The Harriman Alaska Expedition first named many of the surrounding glaciers for American colleges, then named the fjord.

The expedition was organized and sponsored by Edward Henry Harriman of New York who invited about 30 scientific men to go to Alaska aboard the steamer George W. Elder in the summer of 1899 to explore, conduct surveys and collect specimens. Leaving Seattle on July 1, they cruised about 9,000 miles and named several other geographic features, including Harriman Glacier and Fiord, before returning on August 31.

Baltimore Glacier was named later—in 1908—but in the college-naming tradition, by U.S. Grant and D.F. Higgins for "the Woman's College of Baltimore, now Goucher College."

Eliot Glacier, which heads on Mount Marcus Baker and trends seven miles to Harvard Glacier, was named two years later—in 1910—by Lawrence Martin of a National Geographic Society expedition for Charles William Eliot, a former Harvard president. Martin also named Lowell (for Abbot Lawrence Lowell, another Harvard president) and Downer Glacier (for Milwaukee-Downer College for Women in Milwaukee, Wisconsin).

Mount Marcus Baker was named even later—in 1924—by A.H. Brooks for a cartographer with the U.S. Coast and Geodetic Survey and the U.S. Geological Survey.

Just out of the photograph to the left are Barnard and Holyoke glaciers.
(Steve McCutcheon)

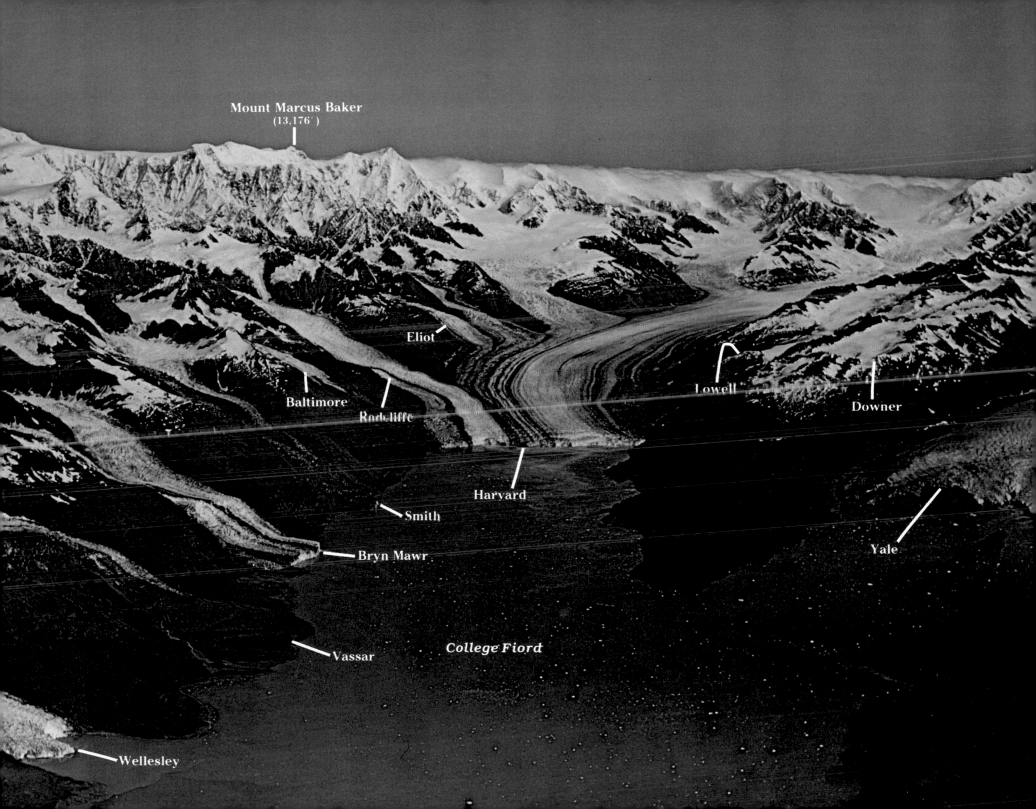

Mount Marcus Baker
(13,176′)

Eliot

Baltimore

Radcliffe

Lowell

Downer

Harvard

Smith

Bryn Mawr

Yale

Vassar

College Fiord

Wellesley

road off the Seward Highway, attracts almost as many sightseers as Mount McKinley.

About 47 miles north of Portage sprawls Anchorage, population about 180,750, Alaska's largest city and hub of commerce, industry, transportation and culture for the region and the state. A fast-growing boom town, Anchorage got its start from railroad construction, grew dramatically with establishment of nearby military facilities during World War II, and continues to expand over the lowland where Knik Arm and Turnagain Arm, the gaping jaws of upper Cook Inlet, converge.

Urban sprawl has pushed Anchorage into Mountain View, Muldoon, Spenard, South Anchorage. Eagle River, a quick drive out the Glenn Highway to just beyond the army's Fort Richardson and the air force's Elmendorf, is a residential retreat for many Anchorage workers. A city bus system, financial services, universities, cultural events, medical facilities, towering hotels and award-winning restaurants. . . . Anchorage has most everything the Lower 48 cities offer and then some. Dog mushers race through downtown streets during the Anchorage Fur Rendezvous, some office workers cross-country ski along a 75-mile network of trails to beat the morning and afternoon traffic jams that can plague the city's main thoroughfare. On some nights the wispy drapes of the northern lights can be seen over Anchorage. And what Lower 48 city can boast wild moose munching on backyard bushes, or a wolf pack in a valley just beyond the city limits?

Anchorage is made up of people from almost everywhere and anywhere. A few are even from Anchorage. Originally part of the homeland of the Tanaina branch of Athabascan Indians, Anchorage has welcomed all.

The Port of Anchorage handles a major portion of the state's marine shipping volume. Several firms run scheduled containership and barge service to the Lower 48.

Downtown Anchorage is a 20-block area of department stores, high-rise hotels and office buildings, shops, theaters, and restaurants. But like all modern cities, shopping malls and businesses are scattered throughout this sprawling town. Many of the city's buildings were part of the flurry of new construction which followed the destructive 1964 earthquake.

Satellite transmissions bring Outside news to Anchorage. Television and radio stations, and two daily newspapers, keep Anchoragites informed.

North of Anchorage the Alaska Range stretches across the horizon. The Talkeetna Mountains rise to the northeast; the broad birch and willow forests of the Susitna lie to the northwest. Spreading out from where the Glenn and George Parks highways converge is the Matanuska Valley, agricultural heartland of Alaska. A variety of crops—both grain and horticultural—grow in the rich soil. The Matanuska Valley has a 120-day growing season, and up to 19 hours of sunlight daily in summer.

South of the Kenai Peninsula lie the 16 major islands of the Kodiak Archipelago. Kodiak is synonymous with bears and fish. Kodiak National Wildlife Refuge covers much of Kodiak Island itself. The brown/grizzly bears for which the island is renowned are especially numerous in the western and southern reaches of the island but they also exist in the north where cattle graze.

Kodiak's streams, some of which can be reached by road, offer excellent trout and salmon fishing. But commercial fishing is king . . . the lifeblood of an economy that harvests millions of pounds of crab, shrimp, halibut, salmon, scallops and herring. Bottom fishing, a new piece of the commercial fishing pie, is certain to play an important role in the future.

Kodiak is one of the largest commercial fishing ports in the United States, and an important transshipment center for cargo bound for the Aleutians, the Alaska Peninsula, and other destinations.

Above
Sea lions swim near Point Elrington at the south end of Elrington Island in Prince William Sound.
(Jana Craighead, reprinted from *ALASKA®* magazine)

Left

The tiny village of Tatitlek, population 68, clings to the shores of Prince William Sound below Copper Mountain, about 40 miles northwest of Cordova.
(Nancy Simmerman)

Lower left

The neatly organized community of Valdez, population 3,279. The town was severely damaged in the 1964 earthquake and its citizens voted to move the townsite to a safer location before rebuilding.
(Steve McCutcheon)

Right

A state ferry and several tour boats take visitors past Columbia Glacier, a major attraction in Prince William Sound. Only the lower 12 miles of the glacier's 34-mile total length can be seen from Columbia Bay.
(Nancy Simmerman)

Left
*Bearberry adds a touch
of red to the tundra carpet of
Little O'Malley Peak in Chugach
State Park.*
(Staff)

Left
*Layers of peaks stack together
in this telephoto view of the
Chugach Mountains, taken
in April from the summit
of O'Malley Peak, not far
from Anchorage in the
Chugach Mountains.*
(John Dancer)

Right
*The Matanuska Glacier extends
27 miles from its head in the
Chugach Mountains to a stream
that flows into the Matanuska
River 46 miles northeast
of Palmer.*
(Ed Cooper)

Aerial view of the Matanuska
Valley, looking north over
Palmer. The Talkeetna
Mountains loom on the horizon
and at center and right is the
Matanuska River.
(Alan C. Paulson)

Left
Peaks of the Alaska Range near Cathedral Spires about 60 miles southwest of the McKinley summit are illuminated by a late evening sun in this photo taken from a small plane flying at 9,000 feet.
(Staff)

Lower left
Four oil drilling platforms are visible in this photo taken in upper Cook Inlet. Gas that is released when the oil is brought to the surface is burned off, or flared.
(Steve McCutcheon)

Left
Five-year-old Andy Grendahl lands his first king salmon at Lake Creek, which flows into the Yentna River 58 miles northwest of Anchorage.
(Jim Thiele)

Right
Aerial view of Anchorage. The downtown shopping area is in the center, bordered on the left by Ship Creek and on the right by the Park Strip, a block-wide and several-block-long greenbelt. Facilities for the Port of Anchorage are at the extreme left. The Chugach Mountains rise in the distance.
(North Pacific Aerial Surveys)

Above
Downtown Anchorage, looking west across Cook Inlet to the peaks of the Aleutian Range. Anchorage is Alaska's largest city and the commercial and transportation center for Southcentral.
(George Herben)

Right
The major winter event for Anchorage, Fur Rendezvous, offers a variety of indoor and outdoor events including world championship sled dog races. Here Roland Lombard, one of the most successful mushers, guides his team along the men's championship course.
(Gary Lackie)

Left
A bore tide surges up Turnagain Arm. Tides can reach 30 feet in six hours along the arm.
(Bob Cellers)

Left
Grasses grow in the tide flats along Turnagain Arm southeast of Anchorage.
(Ed Cooper)

Below
Early morning sun in November lights icebergs in Portage Lake near the head of Turnagain Arm. Portage Glacier is hidden by the fog.
(Nancy Simmerman)

49

Below
The area near Clam Gulch on the Cook Inlet shore of the Kenai Peninsula is a popular spot for clam diggers. The peaks of the Aleutian Range rise in the distance across Cook Inlet.
(Nancy Simmerman)

Left
Seward, on Resurrection Bay, celebrates the Fourth of July in grand style. A grueling run up 3,022-foot Mount Marathon is just one of the events which attracts hundreds of visitors.
(John Warden, reprinted from *The MILEPOST*®)

Right
Kenai Lake extends southwest 24 miles from the Kenai River to the mouth of Snow River, 22 miles northwest of Seward.
(John Warden)

50

Above.
Homer Spit reaches out four and a half miles from the north shore of Kachemak Bay at Homer. Several fishing-related facilities and a small-boat harbor line the shores of the spit.
(Staff)

Right
The fishing community of Seldovia, population 505, spreads out along the east shore of Seldovia Bay, 16 miles southwest of Homer. A state ferry connects the town with other Southcentral/Gulf Coast ports.
(Karen Donelson)

Left
Wildlife in Southcentral is varied and sometimes amusing. These two brown/grizzly bears are relaxing near McNeil River, a state game sanctuary on the west side of Cook Inlet.
(Larry Aumiller)

Below
Midwinter light casts a pinkish glow on Augustine Island in lower Cook Inlet, 70 miles southwest of Homer. The volcanic island last erupted in late January and early February, 1976.
(Art Kennedy, reprinted from *ALASKA®* magazine)

Right
The harbor at Kodiak, one of the top fishing ports in the country.
(Staff)

Interior

*Kayakers paddle
through calm waters of
Wonder Lake in
Denali National Park
and Preserve.
Peaks of the Alaska
Range loom in
the distance.*
(Jim Shives)

For some the Interior is the "real" Alaska. Low rolling hills, braided streams flowing into meandering rivers, forested taiga and treeless tundra, all corralled between the Alaska Range on the south, the Brooks Range on the north, the Canadian border on the east and a transition zone with the Bering Sea coast region on the west.

The Interior is a land of superlatives. On the region's southern border stands Mount McKinley, at 20,320 feet the highest peak on the continent. Alaska's longest river, the Yukon, crosses the region's midsection. The Yukon and its tributaries provided the avenues of exploration which eventually brought trappers and miners into the Interior's immense wilderness.

Low precipitation, wide temperature variations and stagnant air masses typify the continental climate of the region. The mean annual wind speed averages five miles per hour at Fairbanks, where prevailing winds are from the north. In Fairbanks January is the calmest month; May the windiest. In January temperatures in Fairbanks average -11°F; in July the average soars to 60°F. The state's highest temperature, 100°F, was recorded in 1915 at Fort Yukon. Prospect Creek, northeast of Bettles, has the dubious distinction of recording the state's lowest temperature, -80°F, in 1971.

There are two distinct environments in the Interior. In the highlands, below 2,000 feet, and in river valleys, boreal forests (taiga) of white spruce, birch and aspen dominate over stands of balsam poplar and tamarack. In muskeg and bogs, however, the hardy, but stunted, black spruce grows. There are also willow, alder, berries, wild flowers, grasses and sedges.

On the tundra, the region's least productive landscape in terms of plant growth, only those plants that can work their roots into the soil and hang on through cold, heat and wind survive.

A land as vast as the Interior, with many wild areas, can shelter large numbers of big and small mammals, birds and fish. Some of the

prime wildlife habitat has been set aside as national parks, preserves, monuments and wildlife refuges.

Alaska's major tourist attraction—Mount McKinley—lies within 5.7-million-acre Denali National Park and Preserve. The park offers visitors a good chance of seeing wildlife.

On the Interior's eastern border is Yukon-Charley Rivers National Preserve, providing necessary habitat for endangered peregrine falcons, other raptors, waterfowl, bear and moose. Easiest access to the preserve is by boat from Eagle (population 186) on the Yukon River at the end of the Taylor Highway. At the southeastern corner of the Interior along the Alaska Highway is 700,000-acre Tetlin National Wildlife Refuge.

To the north a portion of the central Brooks Range has been set aside as the Gates of the Arctic National Park and Preserve.

Some areas containing crucial wildlife nesting and foraging habitat qualify as national wildlife refuges. Chief among these in the Interior is the Yukon Flats National Wildlife Refuge containing 8,630,000 acres in the vast interior basin, where the mighty river escapes the confines of its temporarily canyon-rimmed course and spreads out over a wide flood plain for 200 miles, creating a great waterfowl breeding area. From there millions of birds—American wigeons, pintails, green-winged teals, scoters, northern shovelers, scaup, canvasbacks, and numerous other species—migrate to four continents. Large (caribou, moose, grizzly and black bears, and wolves) and small (beavers, muskrats, lynx, snowshoe hares) mammals inhabit the flats, and five species of salmon—mostly king and chum—swim through the waterways seeking their spawning grounds.

Passage of the 1980 Alaska National Interest Lands Conservation Act established new wildlife refuges and expanded existing refuges in the Interior. These include the 18-million-acre Arctic National Wildlife Refuge which extends into the northeastern corner of the Interior, and the Kanuti, Koyukuk and Nowitna refuges to the west. A portion of the Innoko refuge also lies within the Interior.

Transportation in the Interior is chiefly by air or water, although in the eastern Interior, roads—the Dalton, Elliott, Steese, Taylor, Richardson, George Parks and Alaska highways—play a major role in the movement of goods and people.

Fairbanks, city population about 25,000, is the focal point for this road system, and serves as the population, commercial, financial and industrial center for the Interior—a region which contains about one-third of Alaska's territory and about one-fifth of its population.

At neighboring North Pole, population 928, a refinery processes more than 30,000 barrels of crude oil per day. The trans-Alaska pipeline passes near Fairbanks and construction activities for the project were coordinated out of the city. The University of Alaska, at College on the edge of Fairbanks, offers a wide variety of programs, specializing in courses related to the northern environment. The renowned Geophysical Institute on the university's campus serves as a leading source of information on northern phenomena. Nearby, too, is the army's Fort Wainwright and Eielson Air Force Base.

With rising metal and fuel prices, mining—by individuals and companies—is once again a profitable occupation in the Fairbanks area. The Usibelli Coal Mine near Healy has been operating since the early part of the century and continues to produce high-quality subbituminous coal.

Increased fur prices have encouraged more year-round residents to run trap lines. Guiding for hunting has always supported some residents of the Interior, and now a shift to guiding for wilderness and photography treks is bringing income to an increasing number of guides.

Subsistence is a way of life for many in the Interior, but occasionally residents supplement their hunting, fishing and trapping with temporary jobs in construction or fire fighting.

Some of the larger settlements, such as Galena (population 805), McGrath (population 343), Bettles (population 94), and Arctic Village (population 111), serve as trading centers and jumping-off points for wilderness excursions.

Southeast of Fairbanks along the Tanana River valley is the agricultural center of the Interior. Commerical crops in the Delta Junction area include barley, oats, and other grains. Agricultural development is also under way in the Nenana area southwest of Fairbanks.

INDEX TO INTERIOR GEOGRAPHIC FEATURES

New names established by the 1980 Alaska National Interest Lands Conservation Act are in parentheses following the old name.

Alaska Highway **G8**
Alaska Railroad **F6**
Alaska Range **H4**
Alatna Hills **C4**
Alatna River **C4**
Allakaket **D4**
Anderson **F6**
Arctic Circle **D**
Arctic Village **B7**

Bettles Field **C5**
Birch Creek **D8**
Black River **D9**
Boundary **G10**
Brooks Range **B5**

Central **E8**
Chalkyitsik **D8**
Chandalar Lake **C6**
Chandalar River **C8**
Chena Hot Springs Road **F7**
Chicken **G9**
Christian River **C7**
Circle **E8**

Dalton Highway **C5**
Davidson Mountains **A9**
Delta Junction **G7**

Eagle **F8**
Elliott Highway **E5**
Evansville **C5**

Fairbanks **F7**
Fortymile River **G9**
Fort Yukon **D8**

Galena **E2**
Gates of the Arctic National Monument (Gates of the Arctic National Park and Preserve) **B4**
George Parks Highway **F6**

Healy **G6**
Hughes **D3**
Huslia **D2**

Innoko National Wildlife Refuge **F1**

John River **C5**

Kaiyuh Mountains **F2**
Kantishna River **G5**
Kanuti National Wildlife Refuge **D4**
Kobuk River **C3**
Koyukuk **E2**
Koyukuk National Wildlife Refuge **E1**
Koyukuk River **E2**
Kuskokwim Mountains **G2**
Kuskokwim River **H2**

Lake Minchumina **G4**
Livengood **E6**

Manley Hot Springs **F5**
McGrath **H2**
Minto **E6**
Mount Deborah **G7**
Mount Doonerak **B5**
Mount Hayes **G7**
Mount Igikpak **C3**
Mount McKinley **H5**
Mount Mckinley National Park (Denali National Park and Preserve) **G5**
Mount Moffitt **G7**

Nenana **F6**
Nenana River **G6**
Nikolai **H3**
North Pole **F7**
North Slope Haul Road **C5**
Northway **H9**

Norutak Lake **C3**
Nowitna National Wildlife Refuge **F3**
Nulato **E1**

Old John Lake **B8**

Philip Smith Mountains **C6**
Porcupine River **C8**

Rampart **E5**
Ray Mountains **E5**
Richardson Highway **G7**
Ruby **F3**

Sheenjek River **C8**
Steese Highway **E8**
Stevens Village **D6**

Tanacross **G9**
Tanana **E4**
Tanana River **F5**
Taylor Highway **G9**
Tetlin **H9**
Tetlin Lake **H9**
Tetlin National Wildlife Refuge **H9**
Tok **H9**
Trans-Alaska Pipeline **D5**

Venetie **C7**
Vunzik Lake **C8**

Walker Lake **C4**
William O. Douglas Arctic Wildlife Range (Arctic National Wildlife Refuge) **A8**
Wiseman **C5**

Yukon-Charley National Monument (Yukon-Charley Rivers National Preserve) **F8**
Yukon Flats **D7**
Yukon Flats National Monument (Yukon Flats National Wildlife Refuge) **C8**
Yukon River **E5**

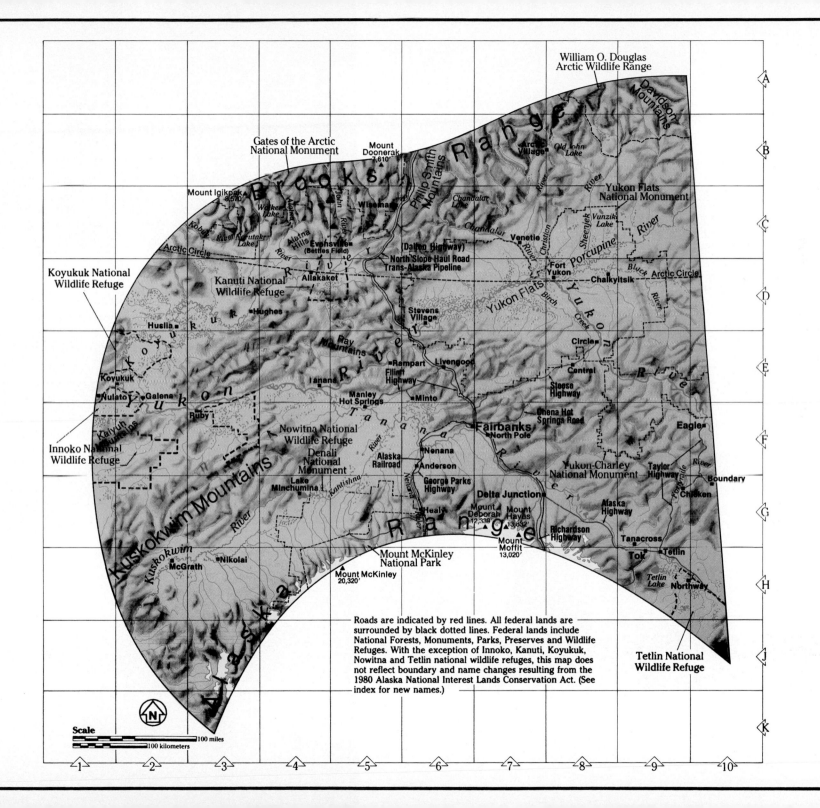

William O. Douglas
Arctic Wildlife Range

Davidson
Mountains

Gates of the Arctic
National Monument

Mount
Doonerak
7,610'

Arctic
Village

Old John
Lake

Brooks Range

Philip Smith Mountains

Mount Igikpak
8,570'

Walker
Lake

John River

Wiseman

Chandalar
Lake

Chandalar River

Yukon Flats
National Monument

Vunziki
Lake

Sheenjek River

Porcupine River

Koyukuk National
Wildlife Refuge

Kobuk River

Norutakr
Lake

Alatna
Hills

Evansville
(Bettles Field)

Venetie

Christian River

Arctic Circle

Fort
Yukon

Black River

Chalkyitsik

Arctic Circle

Kanuti National
Wildlife Refuge

Allakaket

(Dalton Highway)
North Slope Haul Road
Trans-Alaska Pipeline

Huslia

Hughes

Stevens
Village

Yukon Flats

Birch Creek

Yukon River

Koyukuk River

Ray
Mountains

Rampart

Livengood

Circle

Koyukuk

Nulato

Galena

Tanana

Elliott
Highway

Steese
Highway

Central

Yukon River

Ruby

Manley
Hot Springs

Minto

Ohena Hot
Springs Road

Kaiyuh
Mountains

Innoko National
Wildlife Refuge

Nowitna National
Wildlife Refuge

Denali
National
Monument

Tanana River

Alaska
Railroad

Nenana

Anderson

Fairbanks

North Pole

Eagle

Yukon-Charley
National Monument

Taylor
Highway

Fortymile River

Boundary

Lake
Minchumina

Kantishna River

George Parks
Highway

Nenana River

Delta Junction

Mount
Deborah
12,336'

Mount
Hayes
13,832'

Richardson
Highway

Alaska
Highway

Chicken

Kuskokwim Mountains

Healy

Mount
Moffit
13,020'

Alaska Range

Tanacross

Tetlin

Mount McKinley
National Park

Nikolai

McGrath

Kuskokwim River

Mount McKinley
20,320'

Tok

Tetlin
Lake

Northway

Roads are indicated by red lines. All federal lands are
surrounded by black dotted lines. Federal lands include
National Forests, Monuments, Parks, Preserves and Wildlife
Refuges. With the exception of Innoko, Kanuti, Koyukuk,
Nowitna and Tetlin national wildlife refuges, this map does
not reflect boundary and name changes resulting from the
1980 Alaska National Interest Lands Conservation Act. (See
index for new names.)

Tetlin National
Wildlife Refuge

Scale
100 miles
100 kilometers

Below
Of the four species of eagles that inhabit Alaska, by far the most common in the Interior is the golden eagle. It preys chiefly on snowshoe hares, marmots, squirrels, rodents and smaller birds.
(Rick McIntyre)

Right
The Yukon breaks free of its canyon-walled channel when it reaches the Yukon Flats and spreads out over a lowland for the next 200 miles, thus creating the perfect breeding ground for millions of waterfowl.
(Dennis and Debbie Miller)

Above
*Stands such as these of
deciduous birch and aspen mix
with white spruce in many of the
Interior's forests.*
(Robert Langlotz)

Right
*In permafrost areas, pure ice—
often called ice lenses—lies a few
inches below the surface.*
(Steve McCutcheon)

Left
Ice fog, formed when warm air aloft traps colder air near the ground, is a frequent occurrence in Fairbanks in the winter.
(Robert Langlotz)

Above
At first glance the tundra appears as a vast greenish carpet but closer inspection reveals lowbush cranberries, blueberries, lichens, mosses and numerous other plant species.
(Johnny Johnson)

Left
Meandering rivers flow throughout the lowland areas of the Interior. In time, curves in the river's channel are cut off from the main stream and when this happens, oxbow lakes are formed.
(Steve McCutcheon)

63

Right
A reputation for ferociousness leads many animals to avoid the wolverine, a solitary hunter found in isolated reaches of the Interior.
(William Bacon III)

Below
The huge feet of this immature lynx enable the animal to cope handily with deep snow when chasing snowshoe hares.
(Steve McCutcheon)

Below
Grassland in the Interior supports two bison herds, a large herd near Big Delta and a much smaller herd near Farewell in the western Interior.
(Steve McCutcheon)

Right
Largest member of the deer family is the moose, found throughout the Interior. The velvet has been rubbed off the antlers of this young bull but the blood that nourishes the velvet is still visible.
(Martin Grosnick)

Left
Alaska's most famous geographical feature is Mount McKinley, at 20,320 feet the highest peak in North America. This somewhat familiar view is across Wonder Lake, in Denali National Park and Preserve.
(Michio Hoshino)

Below
Sled dogs are an integral part of life at Denali National Park. In summer the dogs demonstrate sled pulling and other skills for visitors. In winter the dogs haul rangers and equipment on back-country patrol.
(Jim Shives)

Right
Mike Wild, out for a day's skiing, found this ice bridge on a glacier east of Mount McKinley.
(Steven Kaufman)

Left
Aerial view of Fairbanks and the Chena River. Fairbanks has grown from a trading post for nearby gold camps to the second-largest city in Alaska. About 58,300 people live within Fairbanks-North Star Borough.
(Steve McCutcheon)

Below
A gold dredge leaves a trail of tailings as it works the dirt near Fairbanks. Felix Pedro's claim just after the turn of the century heralded the beginnings of the Fairbanks mining district.
(Steve McCutcheon)

Left
Fishing, both commercial, which brings in cash, and subsistence, which bring in needed food, keeps many interior residents busy during the summer. Cash catch is primarily king and chum salmon. This fisherman is checking a set net near Rampart on the Yukon River.
(Harry Walker)

Left
Agriculture in the Interior centers around the Tanana River valley southeast of Fairbanks. Crops include barley, oats and wheat. Here a stacker shapes the hay into neat piles near Delta Junction.
(Staff)

Above
Low-hanging sun glances off the trans-Alaska pipeline as it winds past 5,600-foot Mount Wiehl (left) and 4,200-foot Sukakpak Mountain in the Dietrich River valley on the south slope of the Brooks Range.
(Steve McCutcheon)

69

Below
Circle Hot Springs, 29 miles southwest of Circle, became a resort when Franklin Leach developed his 160-acre homestead near the springs. Visiting miners who wanted to bathe in the springs occasionally had to chip the ice off the tent flaps when using the bathhouses.
(Sharon Paul, Staff)

Right
The Yukon flows 1,400 miles through Alaska, much of that across the heartland of the Interior. Boats ranging from large river steamers to the tiniest kayaks and rafts have carried passengers and freight from village to village and to remote sites along the river's shores.
(Sharon Paul, Staff)

Opposite
Nenana, population 592, on the Tanana River has served as a major river boat port for the Interior. The annual Nenana Ice Classic challenges thousands to guess, to the nearest minute, when the Tanana ice will break up at Nenana.
(John and Margaret Ibbotson)

Below
Canoeists paddle near shore on the crystal clear waters of Takahula Lake. Just over the low, forested hills bordering the lake's east shore runs the Alatna River, a major tributary of the Koyukuk River.
(Jim Stuart)

Above
Jumping-off point for the Gates of the Arctic and other points in the central Brooks Range is Bettles Field near the confluence of the Koyukuk and John rivers. The lodge at Bettles Field contains some of the few modern conveniences available in the area.
(Gil Mull)

Right
Caribou skins hang to dry at Arctic Village, on the East Fork of the Chandalar River.
(Dennis and Debbie Miller)

Alaska Peninsula & Aleutians

*Goose banders
search the
lush grasses of
Buldir Island
in the western
Aleutians for
endangered
Aleutian
Canada geese.*
(R.H. Day)

The stone-linked Aleutian Chain forms a slender divider between two of the world's wildest bodies of water, the North Pacific and the stormy Bering Sea, bridging the gap between North America and Asia. Its magnificently faceted, treeless isles are actually crests of an arc of submarine volcanoes, approximately 1,400 miles long and 20 to 60 miles wide, that rise to a maximum height of 9,372 feet above sea level (Shishaldin Volcano on Unimak Island) and 32,472 feet above the ocean floor. On the Pacific side the chain is bordered by the Aleutian Trench, an extraordinary trough more than 2,000 miles long, 50 to 100 miles wide with a maximum depth of more than 25,000 feet where continental plates meet beneath the ocean floor. To the north the relatively shallow Bering Sea slopes downward, forming the world's largest known underwater valley, some 249 miles long with a maximum depth of 10,677 feet.

The Aleutians are the longest archipelago of small islands (124) in the world and the greatest arc of active volcanoes in the United States. The volatile span dates back millions of years and is still in a state of flux. Amak, in the eastern region, surfaced about 7,000 years ago and Bogoslof, which emerged in the late 1700s, is still being shaped by volcanic activity and the elements.

Volcanic eruptions and earthquakes remain a common threat as do the tidal waves and landslides they often spawn. At least 26 of the chain's 57 volcanoes have erupted since 1760. But the remoteness of population centers and the severity of climate still discourage geologists, making the chain one of the very few active areas in the world not cataloged by the International Association of Volcanologists.

On April Fools' Day, 1946, the Aleutians suffered a quake that sent waves more than 100 feet high to nearby Unimak, obliterating Scotch Cap lighthouse and killing five coastguardsmen. Seismic sea waves from this quake swept the Pacific at more than 500 miles per hour.

slamming into Hawaii less than five hours later, killing 159, injuring 163 and causing an estimated $25 million damage.

A seismic warning system was established two years later to protect Hawaiians but seismic work on the Aleutian Chain was not begun in earnest until the 1970s.

The usually conservative U.S. Coast and Geodetic Survey sailing directions declare Aleutian weather the worst in the world. Storm fronts generally move from west to east here but often climatic conditions on the Pacific side differ vastly from those on the Bering side, placing the islands in a continuing weather war. In October of 1977 the remains of tropical storm Harriet slammed into the Aleutians forcing barometric pressure to the lowest ever recorded: 27.35 inches at Adak and off the glass at Atka. Waves from 45 to 50 feet high were reported off Cape Sarichef and several homes were blown off their foundations at Atka.

Measurable precipitation occurs on an average of more than 200 days each year with an annual average of 33.44 inches at Cold Bay on the Alaska Peninsula and 28.85 inches at Shemya in the extreme western Aleutians.

Luckily, Aleutian temperatures are milder than elsewhere in Alaska due to the southerly position and the tempering effect of the surrounding waters. At Shemya temperatures range from 39°F to 53°F in summer and from 28°F to 39°F in winter. The 28.85 inches of precipitation include 57 inches of snow. At Dutch Harbor, near the mainland, temperatures range from 40°F to 60°F in summer and from 27°F to 37°F in winter. The 58 inches of precipitation annually includes 81 inches of snow.

There is little or no permafrost and gardens thrive when unmolested by predators. The islands are treeless except where man has succeeded in nurturing spruce in sheltered valleys. In summer the Aleutians become emerald Edens of grasses studded with a variety of wild flowers.

"The arctic and alpine merge on these islands ... rosy finches and arctic snow buntings nest practically side by side close to sea level," noted biologist Olaus Murie. The chain is a focal point to which animal life has long come from north and south, east and west, and a melting pot for fauna from two continents. Although a full census has yet to be made, more than 230 species of birds have been recorded.

Marine mammals are attracted to the chain by turbulent seas which produce high nutrient concentrates near the surface and support a rich food chain—plankton, fish and shellfish.

Unimak Island is the natural western limit for caribou, brown/grizzly bear, wolf, wolverine, ground squirrel and weasel. Almost all Aleutian land mammals west of the island's borders were introduced by man: foxes, horses, cattle, sheep, caribou and reindeer. Norway rats came with sailing ships in the mid-1800s; the Rat Islands were named for them.

The Aleutians boast the world's largest range of sea mammals: 23 species counting the now-extinct Steller sea cow. The most continually productive whaling ground in Alaska, the chain has 13 species of cetaceans including the giant bottlenose, Bering Sea beaked and Cuvier's beaked whales.

Until the 1940s naturalists feared the island's sea otters might become extinct but a well-observed ban on hunting (the result of a 1911 international treaty) has brought populations back. Fur seals, which migrate through Aleutian waters en route to the Pribilofs, have also made a healthy comeback after exploitation. Sea lions, once sought for their skins, are now thought to be near maximum population limits, and harbor seals, elephant seals and walrus also now come to the area in increasing numbers.

Vitus Bering, discoverer of Alaska, sighted several

A cruise ship rests at anchor near six-mile-long Aghiyuk Island, northernmost of the Semidi Islands.
(Dennis Hellawell)

77

INDEX TO ALASKA PENINSULA & ALEUTIANS GEOGRAPHIC FEATURES

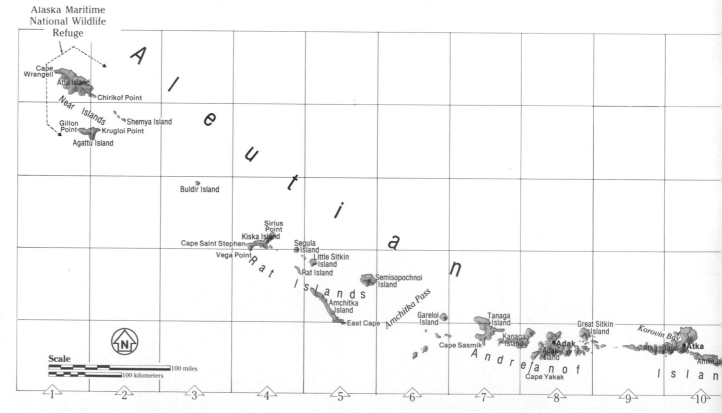

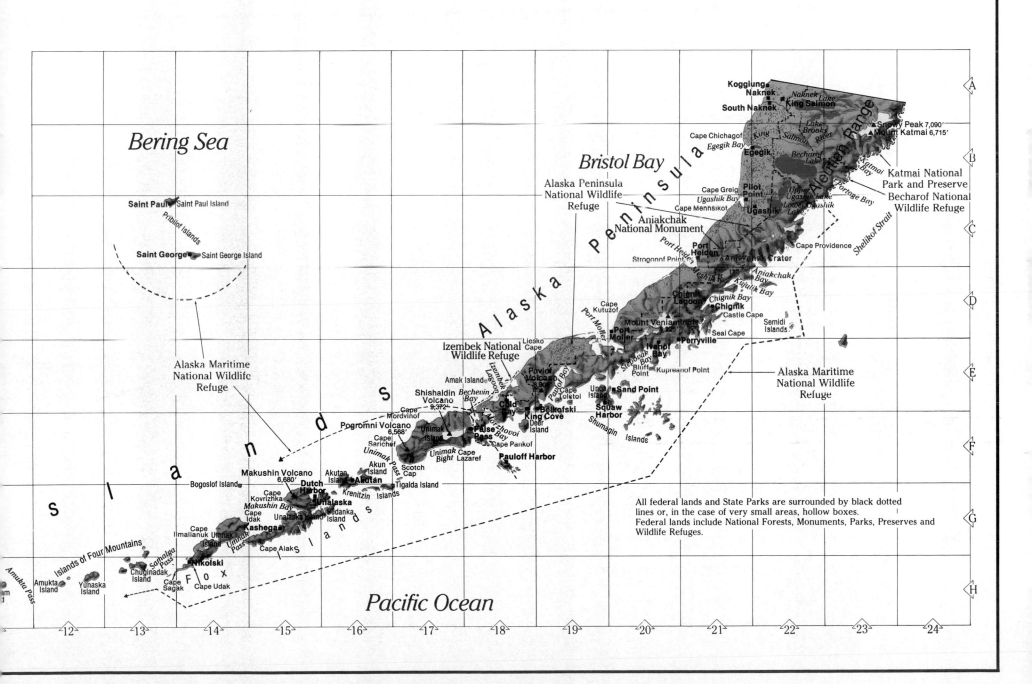

Bering Sea

Koggiunga
Naknek
South Naknek

King Salmon

Naknek *Lake*

Snowy Peak 7,090'
Mount Katmai 6,715'

Cape Chichagof
Egegik Bay
Egegik

Lake Brooks

King *Salmon River*

Becharof Lake

Katmai Bay

Bristol Bay

Katmai National Park and Preserve

Becharof National Wildlife Refuge

Alaska Peninsula National Wildlife Refuge

Cape Greig
Pilot Point
Cape Mennsikof
Ugashik

Ugashik Bay

Upper Ugashik Lake
Lower Ugashik Lake

Portage Bay

Shelikof Strait

Saint Paul • Saint Paul Island

Pribilof Islands

Aniakchak National Monument

Port Heiden

Aniakchak Crater

Cape Providence

Saint George • Saint George Island

Strogonof Point

Port Heiden

Meshik R.

Aniakchak Bay

Kujulik Bay

Chignik Lagoon
Chignik

Chignik Bay

Castle Cape

Alaska Maritime National Wildlife Refuge

Cape Kutuzof

Port Moller

Mount Veniaminof
8,225'

Seal Cape

Semidi Islands

Liesko Cape

Port Moller

Ivanof Bay

Perryville

Stepovak Bay

Izembek National Wildlife Refuge

Amak Island

Izembek Lagoon

Pavlof Volcano
8,905'

Pavlof Bay

Cape Tolstoi

Bluff Point

Kupreanof Point

Alaska Maritime National Wildlife Refuge

Shishaldin Volcano
9,372'

Bechevin Bay

Cold Bay

Belkofski

King Cove

Unga Island

Sand Point

Squaw Harbor

Cape Mordvinof

Pogromni Volcano
6,568'

Unimak Island

Cape Sarichef

Morzhovoi Bay

False Pass

Deer Island

Shumagin Islands

Unimak Pass

Unimak Island
Cape Bight
Scotch Cap
Cape Lazaref

Cape Pankof

Pauloff Harbor

Makushin Volcano
6,680'

Akutan Island
Aleutan

Tigalda Island

Bogoslof Island

Cape Kovrizhka

Dutch Harbor

Krenitzin Islands

Unalaska

All federal lands and State Parks are surrounded by black dotted lines or, in the case of very small areas, hollow boxes.
Federal lands include National Forests, Monuments, Parks, Preserves and Wildlife Refuges.

Makushin Bay

Cape Idak

Unalaska Island

Sedanka Island

Kashegaa

Cape Ilmalianuk Umnak Island

Umnak Pass

Cape Aiak

Islands of Four Mountains

Samalga Pass

Nikolski

Chuginadak Island

Cape Sagak

Cape Udak

Fox

Amukta Island

Yunaska Island

Amukta Pass

Islands

Alaska Peninsula

Aleutian Range

Islands

Fox

Pacific Ocean

of the Aleutian Islands on his homeward voyage in 1741. By 1743 concentrated hunting for seal and sea otter furs had begun. Trade with the Aleuts continued after American purchase in 1867 until depletion of animals forced a moratorium on hunting and the declaration of almost the entire archipelago as a federal wildlife refuge in 1913.

During World War II the western chain was invaded and held by the Japanese and the Aleuts were taken captive or evacuated. A year later Americans won back the ground and began pouring $100 million into fortifications. Thousands of men were based at Adak alone, only to pull out at the war's end leaving the islands almost deserted.

Only about half of the original Aleut population (less than 1,000) returned—the rest were either dead or relocated—and there was little left to attract Outsiders. The mail boat was discontinued in the late 1940s and only occasional plane service connected remote villages. Although there was some fishing-related industry in the Aleutians—a cold storage at Sand Point, Popof Island, and fish processing at King Cove—many traditional villages were never resettled; only Nikolski, Akutan, Atka and False Pass were kept alive by a handful of families who existed mainly by subsistence hunting and fishing.

All military bases were closed with the exception of Adak, which the Army Air Force reduced to housekeeping status. Sprawling facilities at Attu and a smaller unit at Sarichef were transferred to the Coast Guard but manned only by small staffs. During the cold war a top secret military installation was opened at Shemya; DEW line sites were built at Sarichef and Nikolski. Adak was transferred to the navy, which made the base its state headquarters. Adak has since become the chain's largest settlement—at peak times accommodating about 5,000 troops, dependents and support personnel.

There was a building boom at Amchitka during the mid-1960s with the multimillion-dollar Atomic Energy Commission testing program, but most of the work

fell to Outsiders. Area residents protested the experiments and were relieved when the operation closed after three massive tests.

Activity picked up again with enactment in 1976 of a 200-mile fishing limit excluding foreign fleets from American waters. Unalaska, previously not listed in the National Marine Fisheries Service count of dollar values and pounds landed, became the top port in the nation in 1978. Crab catch for that year was worth $99.7 million, and there were 14 processors in operation and half a dozen in neighboring Akutan. Today, Akutan and Unalaska continue to rank among the top 20 U.S. ports in value of commercial landings. The catch is mainly king crab. Tanner crab (marketed as snow crab) is also important, and the bottom fish catch is increasing. There is also fishing for halibut, cod, herring, shrimp and salmon.

Fishing and seafood processing are the principal economic activities of the region, along with the Pribilof Islands fur seal harvest, government and some cattle grazing. Aleut Corporation, the Native corporation formed under the 1971 Alaska Native Land Claims Settlement Act, manages some 11,000 square miles of land, extending southwest from the Alaska mainland.

Unalaska is the largest community in the Aleutian Islands census area, with a population of 1,944. (Total population of the region is about 8,600.) Other sizable communities are Sand Point (population 697), Saint Paul (population 591), King Cove (population 513), and Akutan (population 189). The remainder of the Aleutian Chain's Aleut inhabitants are settled mainly in the villages of Atka, Nikolski and False Pass.

Fresh snowfall glistens on the 4,800-foot Aghileen Pinnacles near Cold Bay at the tip of the Alaska Peninsula. The peaks on the horizon are, from left, Frosty, 5,784 feet and on the mainland; Roundtop, 6,140 feet, Isanotski, 8,025 feet, and Shishaldin, 9,372 feet, all on Unimak Island.
(John Sarvis)

Transportation to and among the Aleutians is infrequent and expensive. Rough flying weather and extraordinary operational costs due to small populations combine to give Reeve Aleutian Airways the distinction of flying the most expensive air miles in America. Freight service by sea is irregular and there is no inter-island marine transport system. The Alaska Marine Highway, southwestern system, does have limited summer ferry service to the Aleutian ports of Sand Point and Dutch Harbor, and the Alaska Peninsula ports of Chignik, King Cove and Cold Bay.

The Aleutians' remoteness has been a double-edged sword: it has inhibited growth and development, but has also helped preserve the peace and wild beauty of the islands. Most of the chain remains a wildlife sanctuary, accounting for the majority of acreage in the Alaska Maritime National Wildlife Refuge, a 4.5-million-acre refuge encompassing the coastal waters of Alaska. Most of these lands are extremely rugged and inaccessible, attracting only a few hardy bird watchers (the refuge contains habitat for about 75 percent of the state's total marine bird population).

The Alaska Peninsula's parks, preserves, monuments and refuges are less remote. Katmai National Park and Preserve, established as a national monument in 1918, is reached from Anchorage by scheduled air service to King Salmon, then by road or floatplane to the park. Katmai was set aside to preserve the Valley of Ten Thousand Smokes, which was created by volcanic action in the 1912 eruption of Novarupta. Development includes two lodges, a campground and fishing camp, with four-wheel-drive van tours out to the Valley of Ten Thousand Smokes.

The Alaska Peninsula has been a major big game hunting area for many years, especially for the brown/grizzly bears found in this region. The bears' habitat is protected, either as park, preserve, monument or refuge, along the entire peninsula from Katmai south through the Alaska Peninsula National Wildlife Refuge.

Above
A brown/grizzly bear waits for his next salmon dinner in Katmai National Park and Preserve. The glaucous-winged gulls in the background will readily clean up any scraps left by the bear.
(Martin Grosnick)

Right
On June 6, 1912, 2.5 cubic miles of ash was ejected from Novarupta volcano near Mount Katmai in what some consider to be the second-greatest volcanic eruption in recorded history. More than 40 square miles of the valley near the eruption site were covered with ash, sometimes to depths of 300 feet. This valley was named Valley of Ten Thousand Smokes because there were so many fumaroles still emitting vapors when scientists first arrived to explore the eruption site. The ground has since cooled.
(Michio Hoshino)

Created in 1960, Izembek National Wildlife Refuge on the Alaska Peninsula contains 320,893 acres. The continent's entire brant population feeds here as do many other species of waterfowl. These three photos were all taken in the refuge. From the top, a harbor seal resting on a sand bar at low tide near Cape Glazenap at the west entrance to Applegate Cove. / Flocks of sanderlings and rock sandpipers flying along a beach at Neumann Island. / Barren Ground caribou bulls, their antlers still covered with velvet, at Moffett Point. (All photos by John Sarvis; center photo reprinted from *ALASKA®* magazine)

Left
At the time of the 1960 census count, 41 persons lived in False Pass. In 1970, the number had risen to 62. The salmon cannery was closed and there was little to stir the village's economy. The cannery was eventually reopened and now the 70 inhabitants of False Pass share in the fishing economy of the eastern Aleutians.
(Augie Kochuten)

Below
Glaucous-winged gulls gather on the beach at Cape Sarichef on Unimak Island.
(John Sarvis)

Above
Tundra in the Aleutians harbors numerous berry species. This wild strawberry matures in the tundra near Cape Sarichef on Unimak Island.
(John Sarvis)

Dutch Harbor, combined population with Unalaska, 1,944, viewed from 1,589-foot Mount Ballyhoo, on Amaknak Island. The village of Unalaska, traditionally Aleut, is in the background, across the bay from Dutch Harbor. The fishing economy of the eastern Aleutians centers around Dutch Harbor.
(Bob Nelson, reprinted from *ALASKA*® magazine)

Above
In 1975 Unalaska was not even recorded in the National Marine Fisheries Service count of dollars and pounds landed for U.S. fishing ports. In 1976 the Aleutian community surpassed Kodiak for the number two spot nationally with a crab catch of $48.3 million. Today, Unalaska and nearby Akutan continue to rank among the top 20 U.S. ports in value of commercial landings. Here the Ocean Leader out of Dutch Harbor fights heavy seas while her crew tries to land king crab.
(Sally Ede Bishop, reprinted from *Fisheries of the North Pacific*)

Right
This underwater photo shows a pod of juvenile king crabs congregated on the sea floor near Unalaska. Podding behavior is thought to be for protection and is seldom seen among adult crabs.
(Bob Nelson)

Left

The village of Saint Paul, population about 600, on the island of Saint Paul in the Pribilofs. The five islands of the Pribilof group—Saint Paul, Saint George, Walrus, Sea Lion Rock and Otter—are about 300 miles off the Alaska mainland in the Bering Sea. Residents of the islands are mostly Aleuts who live in two main villages, Saint Paul and Saint George. (Susan Hackley Johnson, reprinted from *ALASKA*® magazine)

Below

A blowing snowstorm partially obscures northern fur seals at their rookery on Saint Paul Island. (Mark Kelley)

Below

In Alaska the red-legged kittiwake, a member of the gull family, breeds only in the Pribilofs and on Buldir and Bogoslof islands in the Aleutians. (Robert Schulmeister)

Below
*Fumes and vapor rise
from 5,675-foot Mount Cleveland
at the west end of Chuginadak
Island, largest of the Islands of
Four Mountains group.*
(Bob Nelson)

Right
*Nikolski, population 50, clusters
around Nikolski Bay near the
west end of Unmak Island.
Benefits from the fishing activity
farther east have not reached
Nikolski and many men must
still work away from the village.*
(Lael Morgan, Staff, reprinted from
ALASKA GEOGRAPHIC®)

Left

An arctic fox in its summer pelage on Kiska Island. In winter this species becomes snowy white. Arctic foxes were introduced to many of the islands during the fox-farming era from the 1880s to the 1930s. When fox farming was no longer profitable, the animals were released to fend for themselves. This, in turn, played havoc with other wildlife species, especially ground-nesting birds. Foxes have been eliminated from a few islands to encourage restoration of decimated bird populations.
(R.H. Day)

Left

Among the most feared marine predators are killer whales. This family (the male has the larger dorsal fin) is searching for prey between Agattu and Buldir islands in the western Aleutians.
(John Sarvis)

Right

The Kamchatka rhododendron, which grows to five inches or more, is found at sea level and on alpine meadows of the Aleutians, Kodiak and the Alaska Peninsula.
(R.H. Day)

Below
Twisted metal grids from an abandoned airfield lie partially buried in the sands of Atka Island, one of the Andreanof group of Aleutian Islands.
(Kevin Hekrdle)

Right
The Aleut village of Atka stands about 120 miles northeast of Adak on the shore of Nazan Bay on Atka Island. One of the most isolated communities in Alaska, the village's approximately 92 residents fish for salmon in the fall and halibut and cod year-round.
(Kevin Hekrdle)

Above
Trees are not indigenous to the Aleutians. This small cluster was planted during World War II on Adak Island and is known as Adak National Forest.
(Susan Schulmeister)

Left
Bald eagles are right at home among the craggy cliffs that dominate much of the Aleutian coastline. This eagle was photographed at Adak Island.
(Michael Gordon)

Bering
Sea Coast

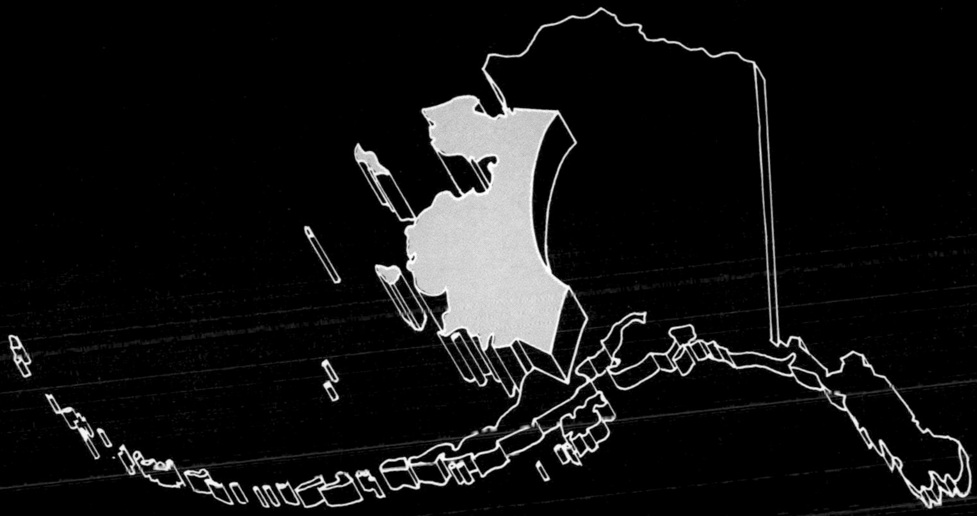

*Solid ice
crowds the
Bering Sea coast
much of the
year. When
breakup does
come, leads
(areas of open
water) form
in the ice
through which
migrating marine
mammals pass.*
(Steve Leatherwood)

The Bering Sea coast region of western Alaska, bordered on the north by Kotzebue Sound (an arm of the Chukchi Sea) and on the south by Bristol Bay, extends inland in a convex curve from the Arctic Circle to Telequana Lake, then south to the Katmai National Park and Preserve boundary and west to the Kvichak River outlet into Bristol Bay.

Just south of Kotzebue Sound, 200-mile-long Seward Peninsula reaches toward Siberia. The peninsula's tip, Cape Prince of Wales, points seaward to Little Diomede Island, a mere three miles from Big Diomede Island, which is Soviet territory. The Kigluaik, Bendeleben, Darby and other mountains break the terrain of the peninsula's southern half while to the north, the flatlands are etched with countless ponds, lakes, inlets and occasional uplands. The Selawik Hills, summit 3,307 feet, rise in the peninsula's northeast corner.

Norton Sound, a 125-mile arm of the Bering Sea, abuts the Nulato Hills south of the Seward Peninsula. The mighty Yukon River curves around the hills from the east and, with the Kuskokwim River to the south, deposits enough silt to form one of the world's major coastal flood plains, the 200-mile-long and 250-mile-wide Yukon-Kuskokwim Delta.

Even farther south the Kilbuck and Ahklun mountains and the more extensive Kuskokwim Mountains reach the sea of Cape Newenham. This mountainous spine separates the delta from Bristol Bay. The lowland surrounding the bay, intersected by the Nushagak and Kvichak rivers, ties the long tail of the Alaska Peninsula to the rest of western Alaska.

Offshore, three major island groups rise above the shallow Bering Sea floor. Saint Lawrence is home for more than 800 Siberian Yup'ik Eskimos. Closer to the mainland, across Etolin Strait from the delta, lies Nunivak Island. Saint Matthew Island and smaller Hall Island lie in the central Bering Sea, midway between Saint Lawrence and the Pribilofs.

The northern portion of the Bering Sea coast borders the Arctic and is subject to the severe climate of the Far North. Long, harsh winters with temperatures ranging from five degrees below to the low twenties are common. In summer the thermometer reads from the low forties to the low sixties. Farther south temperatures moderate a bit. Highs in the thirties to lows around zero are recorded in winter; mid-thirties to mid-sixties are average summer temperatures.

Wind contributes significantly to the region's weather and some areas are seldom without a breeze. North of Bristol Bay rain and snow occur more frequently along the coast than farther inland. Near the bay, however, the opposite is true; precipitation along the coast averages less than farther inland where the highlands are influenced by the moist marine air from Cook Inlet and the Gulf of Alaska.

Transportation along the Bering Sea coast, as in much of Alaska, is by planes and boats in summer, and planes and snow machines in winter. However, there is renewed interest in sled dogs—the Iditarod Trail Sled Dog Race, which begins in Anchorage, crosses the region and terminates in Nome—and higher fuel costs for snow machines may lead to a resurgence of sled dog travel.

Tundra—either wet or upland—characterizes most of the region's vegetation. Grasses, sedges, mosses and lichens and a multitude of wild flowers cover the ground, and scrub willows and alder reach above the tundra. Upriver on the Yukon are stands of white spruce and balsam poplar. Inland on the Kuskokwim River, birch and spruce maintain a tenuous hold in the poor soil. Approaching Bristol Bay the low tundra gives way to thickly forested hillsides . . . some 2.7 million acres in the Bristol Bay area are classified as forest lands.

Although fishing is the backbone of the mainly subsistence economy that predominates in the Bering Sea coast region, reindeer are becoming increasingly important. Several thousand reindeer are herded on the Seward Peninsula, and the village of Stebbins maintains a herd on Stuart Island near the mouth of the Yukon. Additional herds roam Saint Lawrence, Nunivak and Hagemeister islands, as well as the hills around Unalakleet.

Support services for herding, such as helicopter rental, and harvesting antlers for processing into medicinal compounds to be sold in the Orient, employ many villagers on a temporary basis and provide substantial cash income for the herds' owners.

Trade center for the Seward Peninsula is Nome (population about 3,000), a booming gold rush town at the turn of the century and today the administrative center for the peninsula. Gold is still an influence in the community, and Alaska Gold Company dredges—considered major attractions by tour companies—are mining the nearby hills.

In the Bering Sea, 130 miles southwest of Nome, lies Alaska's fourth-largest island, Saint Lawrence, whose Eskimo residents follow Siberian Yup'ik ways. Villagers at the island's two communities, Gambell (population 480) and Savoonga (population 530), decided not to participate in the Alaska Native Claims Settlement Act. Instead they chose to keep their 1.2-million-acre reservation and move forward without government cash allotments. Subsistence and a fledgling tourist industry sustain the island's economy.

The area from Unalakleet north is inhabited mainly by Inupiat Eskimos, who rely mostly on subsistence, although state and federal government agencies provide some temporary jobs.

South of Norton Sound and stretching 250 miles to Kuskokwim Bay and inland 200 miles to the Kuskokwim Mountains, is the Yukon-Kuskokwim Delta, a sandy, loamy, fan-shaped area formed mostly by centuries of deposits from the Yukon River. The delta is extremely fertile and supports abundant plant and animal life. The delta is also wet—not only do the

INDEX TO
BERING SEA COAST
GEOGRAPHIC FEATURES

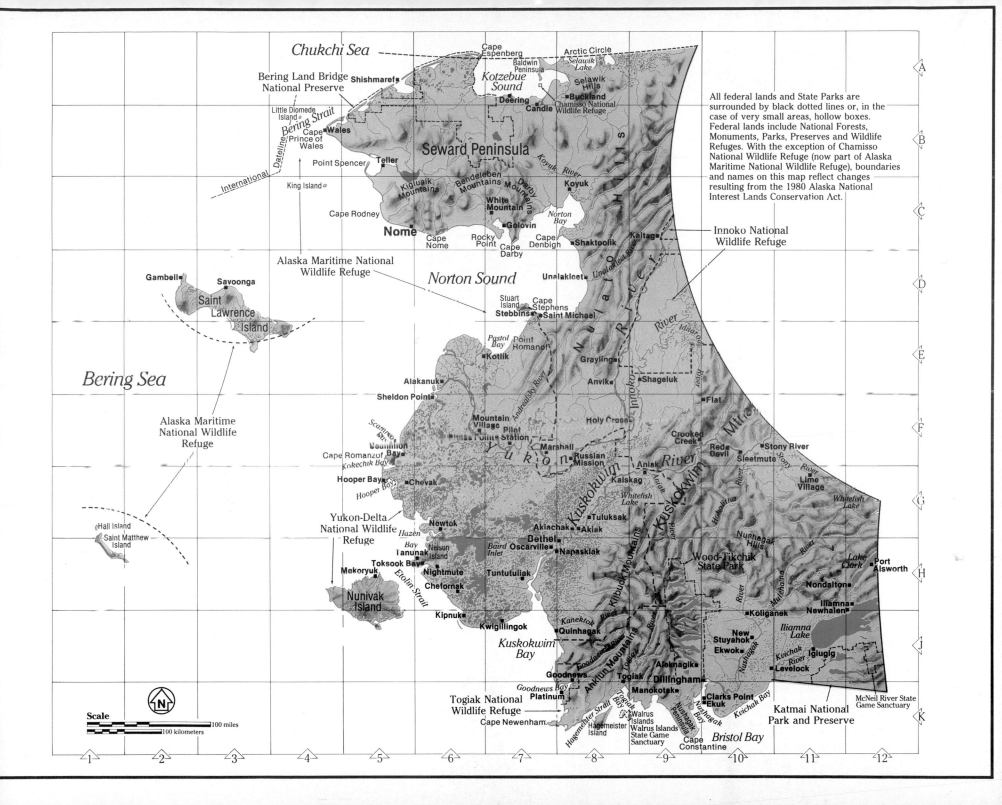

Chukchi Sea

Cape Espenberg

Arctic Circle

Baldwin Peninsula

Selawik Lake

Bering Land Bridge National Preserve

Shishmaref

Kotzebue Sound

Selawik Hills

Buckland

Deering

Candle

Chamisso National Wildlife Refuge

Little Diomede Island

Wales

Bering Strait

Cape Prince of Wales

Seward Peninsula

Koyuk River

Point Spencer

Teller

Dateline

International

King Island

Kigluaik Mountains

Bendeleben Mountains

Darby Mountains

Koyuk

Cape Rodney

White Mountain

Norton Bay

Nome

Golovin

Cape Nome

Rocky Point

Cape Darby

Cape Denbigh

Shaktoolik

Kaltag

Innoko National Wildlife Refuge

Alaska Maritime National Wildlife Refuge

Norton Sound

Unalakleet

Unalakleet River

Nulato Hills

River

Idaarod

Stuart Island

Cape Stephens

Stebbins

Saint Michael

Pastol Bay

Point Homanof

Grayling

River

Bering Sea

Kotlik

Anvik

Shageluk

Alakanuk

Andreafsky River

Sheldon Point

Flat

Innoko River

Mountain Village

Holy Cross

Pilot Station

Alaska Maritime National Wildlife Refuge

Scammon Bay

Crooked Creek

Red Devil

Stony River

Hall Island

Saint Matthew Island

Marshall

Russian Mission

Sleetmute

Mtns

Yukon

Gambell

Savoonga

Saint Lawrence Island

Cape Romanzof

Kokechik Bay

Hooper Bay

Chevak

Hooper Bay

Kaiskag

Kuskokwim River

Aniak

Aniak River

Lime Village

Whitefish Lake

Whitefish Lake

Yukon-Delta National Wildlife Refuge

Newtok

Tuluksak

Kuskokwim

River

Stony River

Holitna

River

Hazen Bay

Akiachak

Akiak

Nushagak Hills

Nelson Island

Baird Inlet

Dethel

Oscarville

Napaskiak

River

Tanunak

Wood-Tikchik State Park

Lake Clark

Port Alsworth

Mekoryuk

Nightmute

Tuntutuliak

Toksook Bay

Etolin Strait

Chefornak

Kilbuck Mountains

Nondalton

Nunivak Island

River

Mulchatna

River

Iliamna

Kipnuk

Koliganek

Newhalen

Kanektok River

New Stuyahok

Iliamna Lake

Kwigillingok

Quinhagak

Togiak River

Ekwok

Nushagak

Kvichak River

Iguigig

Kuskokwim Bay

Aleknagik

Levelock

Goodnews River

Ahklun Mountains

Togiak

Dillingham

Goodnews

Goodnews Bay

Platinum

Manokotak

Clarks Point

Kvichak Bay

Togiak National Wildlife Refuge

Togiak Bay

Ekuk

McNeil River State Game Sanctuary

Cape Newenham

Hagemeister Strait

Hagemeister Island

Walrus Islands

Walrus Islands State Game Sanctuary

Cape Constantine

Nushagak Peninsula

Katmai National Park and Preserve

Bristol Bay

All federal lands and State Parks are surrounded by black dotted lines or, in the case of very small areas, hollow boxes. Federal lands include National Forests, Monuments, Parks, Preserves and Wildlife Refuges. With the exception of Chamisso National Wildlife Refuge (now part of Alaska Maritime National Wildlife Refuge), boundaries and names on this map reflect changes resulting from the 1980 Alaska National Interest Lands Conservation Act.

Scale

100 miles

100 kilometers

A
B
C
D
E
F
G
H
J
K

1 2 3 4 5 6 7 8 9 10 11 12

Yukon and Kuskokwim rivers meander across this broad plain, but there are innumerable streams, sloughs, ponds and lakes, in addition to vast tidal flats. These wetlands are one of the most significant waterfowl breeding areas in North America, and some 19.6 million acres of the delta are included in the Yukon Delta National Wildlife Refuge.

Bethel, heart of the delta, and western Alaska's largest community (population 3,549), serves as its commercial and administrative headquarters. Goods and passengers are flown or barged to Bethel, then transshipped to the villages on bush planes, small barges and shallow-draft boats.

Subsistence, supplemented by dollars from commercial fishing for salmon, is the way of life for most delta residents. Salmon is caught in the summer, and dried and stored for winter. In winter, residents fish through the ice for burbot, sheefish, whitefish, pike and blackfish. Subsistence hunters harvest game, including ptarmigan, snowshoe hare, beaver, moose and caribou, in addition to substantial numbers of geese, ducks and lesser sandhill cranes, plus some seals, walrus, sea lions and beluga whales.

South and east of Kuskokwim Bay and around the corner from Cape Newenham is Bristol Bay, where the economy has traditionally been based on the sea—primarily the salmon industry, although the smaller populations of sheefish and whitefish are significant. Streams and rivers flowing into the bay nourish the largest red salmon spawning grounds in the world.

The Nushagak River system produces the area's major pink salmon run. The Nushagak flows some 240 miles southwest from its headwaters, emptying into Nushagak Bay 3 miles south of Dillingham. Supplies for this fishery, as well as for those destined for most of the villages, funnel through Dillingham (population 1,670), at the confluence of the Wood and Nushagak rivers. Dillingham is also the major center for fish processing in the bay area.

Above
Bull walrus gather under a pinnacle at a point on Round Island. The island is the only known hauling-out spot used exclusively by breeding bulls.
(Brian Milne, reprinted from *ALASKA*® magazine)

Opposite
Wales, population about 140, is at the western tip of the Seward Peninsula. Once one of the largest Inupiat Eskimo villages, residents of Wales today rely on fishing, hunting, reindeer herding and temporary work with various government agencies.
(Mark McDermott)

Left
During summer many Nome residents move to fish camp to catch and dry this staple of the northern diet. Salmon enter several rivers, both east and west of Nome, on the way to spawning streams.
(Jerrianne Lowther)

Above
Jason Hurold, with an expression discouraging all intruders, clears away the ice from his fishing hole in a slough near Unalakleet.
(Jim Simmen)

Right
Henry Oyoumick picks Dolly Varden from a net strung underneath the ice of the Unalakleet River.
(Jim Greenough)

Below
Thousands of reindeer graze on the Seward Peninsula and eastern Norton Sound. Sales of reindeer meat and by-products provide needed income in some areas. The antlers are sold in the Orient for medicinal purposes and the meat and hides from the winter butchering are consumed locally. This herd grazes near Candle not far from the northern coast of the peninsula.
(George Herben)

Right
Corralled reindeer wait their turn to have their antlers clipped at Nome. Selling of antlers brings thousands of dollars into the villages.
(Mark Rauzon)

Far right
Nome, population about 3,000, serves as the commercial center for the Seward Peninsula. Saloons, gift shops, cafes, a drugstore, appliance store, grocery stores and Alaska Commercial Company department store line Nome's main street.
(Penny Rennick, Staff)

Top
A "grizzly" shakes larger rocks from the dirt at this gold mine near the Casadepaga River northeast of Nome. A sluice box attached to the grizzly separates the heavier gold from the gravel. Getting heavy equipment to an isolated mine can be a challenge. This equipment arrived at Nome by barge, and then was trucked to the mine 70 miles away.
(Harry Walker)

Above
Numerous dredges—both working and abandoned—are stationed in the hills around Nome. At the turn of the century Nome was booming. Later the community languished for many years because the price of gold was not high enough to allow profitable extraction. Now, however, the dredges of Alaska Gold Company are once again mining the rich deposits still abundant in the area.
(Penny Rennick, Staff)

Above
Some areas of the Bering Sea coast are swept almost constantly by winds. These hardy residents of Toksook Bay, population 333, on the Yukon-Kuskokwim Delta must brave the elements just to move around their village.
(John McDonald)

Left
The mail plane, lifeline of bush Alaska, carries not only the mail but also visitors, supplies, equipment and special surprises such as Christmas presents. These villagers gather around a mail plane waiting at Toksook Bay.
(John McDonald)

Left
Photographer Harry Walker commemorated the last morning of his trip down the Yukon by taking this photo of his canoe tied to a piece of driftwood stuck into the mud of the Yukon-Kuskokwim Delta between Mountain Village and Alakanuk.

Below
Meandering rivers and a multitude of lakes characterize the Yukon-Kuskokwim Delta. Most of this huge delta is included in the Yukon Delta National Wildlife Refuge.
(Jerry L. Hout, reprinted from *ALASKA GEOGRAPHIC®*)

Left
*The fresh waters around Bristol
Bay nourish the largest red
salmon population in the world.*
(Steve McCutcheon)

Right
*Mrs. Simeon Bartman of
Manokotak sets aside the pinkish
orange roe as she
cleans salmon on this
Bristol Bay beach.*
(Lael Morgan, Staff, reprinted from
ALASKA GEOGRAPHIC®)

Arctic

The Arctic is separated from the rest of Alaska by an invisible line that runs west along the crest of the Brooks Range to Mount Igikpak, near the head of the Noatak River, then curves south past the village of Kobuk to the Arctic Circle and extends west to reach the Chukchi Sea just south of Kotzebue.

The Brooks Range is named for Alfred Brooks (1871-1924), chief Alaskan geologist for the U.S. Geological Survey for more than 20 years. Length of the range from the Canadian border to the Chukchi Sea is 600 line-of-sight miles; however, a measurement of the crest of the range as it twists and turns across the state is 720 miles. The Brooks Range rises in Yukon Territory in the Barn Mountains, the British Mountains and the Buckland Hills. In Alaska, and from east to west, the range encompasses the Davidson Mountains, Romanzof Mountains—the highest and widest portion of the range—the Sadlerochit and Shublik mountains, Philip Smith and Endicott mountains. The Schwatka group, which harbors the Arrigetch Peaks and Mount Igikpak, merge with the Baird and De Long mountains at the western end of the range.

Gently sloping foothills slip from the mountain peaks to the arctic coastal plain. These are essentially rocky slopes cut by rivers which flow to broad deltas along the coast. The Colville River, largest drainage system in the Arctic, joins with the Canning, Sagavanirktok and numerous other rivers to carry rain and snowmelt northward. The Noatak and Kobuk drain the Arctic's western and southwestern reaches.

Strong winds, cold temperatures and low precipitation characterize the arctic climate zone. The Beaufort and Chukchi seas moderate the climate somewhat but temperatures at Barrow, near the northernmost extension of North America, average between 30°F and 40°F in July and August and between -15°F and -18°F in January and February. Temperature inversions are common throughout the Arctic. The cooling trend of rising air masses is reversed

by atmospheric conditions and colder air is trapped near the ground. If air pollution is present under these conditions, its effect is accentuated.

Permafrost, beginning just a few inches under the surface and extending down to 2,000 feet, underlies most of the Arctic. Tundra and bog soils are most common because permafrost impedes drainage. Disturbing the plant cover brings about thawing of the permafrost which, in turn, leads to erosion. Soil erosion along tracked vehicle routes in the Arctic was found to be particularly damaging, so travel is restricted to winter or vehicles are equipped with giant, low-pressure tires which have little or no effect on the landscape.

The region's vegetation consists of several varieties of tundra. Higher elevations support alpine tundra:

lichens, grasses, sedges, some herbs such as mountain avens and saxifrage. Moss campion grows on drier talus slopes. Cotton grass, mosses, lichens, dwarf birch and willows cover the foothills. Sedges, mosses, cotton grass and lousewort predominate on the boggy plain, and high brush vegetation, typified by willow and alder, grows along major river flood plains.

While many square miles are required to sustain large mammals in the Arctic, numerous species including moose, wolves, brown/grizzly bears, and Dall sheep—do make their homes on the northern tundra. Caribou, grouped into two major herds—Western Arctic and Porcupine—roam all but the rockiest slopes of the Brooks Range. Smaller mammals—wolverines, weasels, a few river otters, snowshoe hares, lynx, shrews, lemmings and voles—

also live in the Arctic. On the coastal plain the ranges of the arctic fox and red fox overlap. After being hunted out of Alaska, musk ox were reintroduced to Nunivak Island, where the herd eventually thrived, and then transplanted to the mainland. In this region, musk ox occur on the arctic slope around Kavik and on the seacoast near Cape Thompson. Many bird species migrate to the Arctic to breed and raise their young, although few species overwinter here.

Millions of acres of land in this region have been set aside as monument, preserve, park or refuge. Cape Krusenstern National Monument on the Chukchi Sea coast contains ancient beach fronts created by ocean currents and storms. Artifacts dating back thousands of years have been unearthed from these beach ridges. East from the sea are Noatak National Preserve, Kobuk Valley National Park and Gates of the Arctic National Park and Preserve. Arctic National Wildlife Refuge encompasses 18 million acres in the northeastern corner of the state.

The frigid waters of the Beaufort and Chukchi seas support populations of polar bears, walrus, bowhead and beluga whales, and bearded and ringed seals. In the short summer months when the ice retreats from the coast, harbor seals, harbor porpoises, and killer and gray whales pass by. Rarer species of great whales—the fin, sei, and little piked—also have been reported in Chukchi waters.

Transportation in the Arctic is chiefly by boat and small plane in summer and by plane and snow machine in winter. Dog teams, once the only form of transportation in this region, are still used by residents, either out of preference or necessity. Once a year each summer a fleet of tug-pulled barges from the Lower 48 brings supplies and equipment to coastal villages and the oil-drilling operations at Prudhoe.

Few settlements have been established in the Arctic. Barrow (population about 2,500) serves as the trade center for the North Slope Borough, an area which includes several smaller communities—among

Below
Polygonal forms created by the interaction of vegetation, soil, and the expansion and contraction of the shallow layer of earth above the permafrost characterize much of the North Slope's tundra.
(Steve McCutcheon)

Opposite
Ice wedges thrust out from surrounding permafrost form pingos, the only significant natural elevations on the coastal plain north of the Brooks Range.
(Steve McCutcheon)

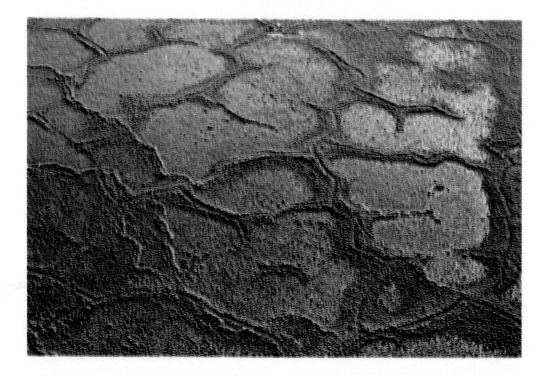

them, Wainwright, Point Hope, Atkasook, Nuiqsut, Anaktuvuk Pass and Kaktovik—and the oil complex at Prudhoe Bay. Commerce among villages in the southwestern Arctic revolves around Kotzebue (population 2,250) in the Kobuk census area. From Kotzebue supplies are shipped to Kobuk, Shungnak, Ambler, Kiana and Noorvik in the Kobuk River valley; Noatak in the Noatak River valley; Kivalina along the coast; Selawik; and other smaller villages.

Oil and subsistence provide the majority of economic support for the Arctic. The Prudhoe Bay oil field discovery was confirmed in 1968 and the 800-mile-long pipeline connecting Prudhoe Bay with the marine terminal at Valdez began operation in 1977. Development of the Prudhoe Bay oil fields and related construction created jobs for many arctic residents and provided the economic stimulus for new houses, schools, hospitals and civic buildings. Substantial hydrocarbon reserves are believed to exist in the Beaufort Sea, and exploration and development continues with major companies such as Sohio, Mobil and BP Alaska drilling exploration wells.

Residents of the smaller villages rely on subsistence and temporary work, usually in construction or government projects. Caribou are important to inland Eskimos, while coastal villagers depend on fish and marine mammals, such as bearded seals, walrus and beluga whales. Before restrictions were placed on hunting the polar bear, Kotzebue was known as the polar bear capital of the world.

Oil does not dominate the economy of Kotzebue and its trading region as it does farther north. Commercial fishing, trapping, fur buying and tourism generate income for this part of the Arctic. NANA, the Native regional corporation of northwestern Alaska, oversees the largest reindeer herd in Alaska, marketing the antlers in the Orient and selling the meat locally. The NANA-operated Museum of the Arctic contains a jade manufacturing operation, displays and demonstrations of Native crafts and skills, and a diorama of Alaska wildlife.

INDEX TO ARCTIC GEOGRAPHIC FEATURES

New names established by the 1980 Alaska National Interest Lands Conservation Act are in parentheses following the old name.

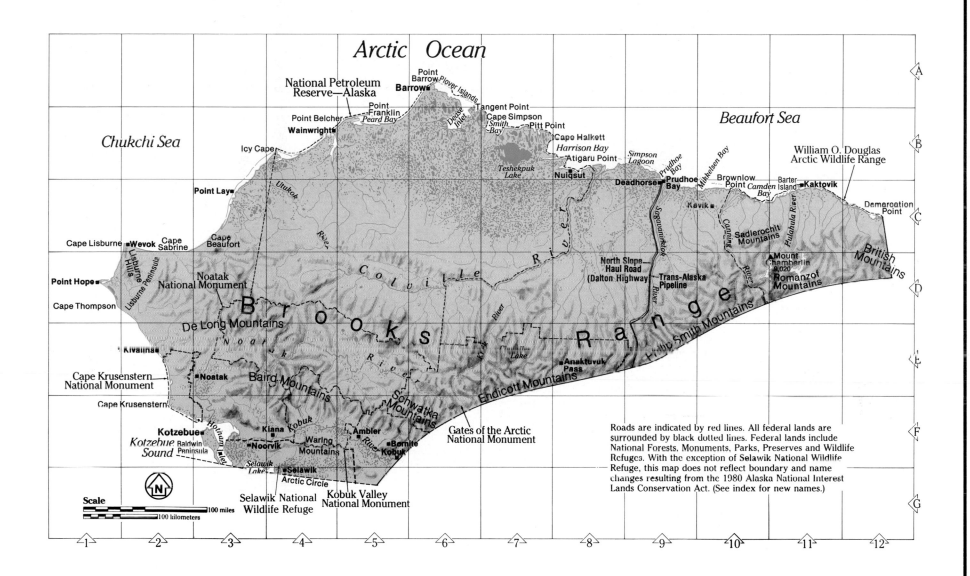

Arctic Ocean

Chukchi Sea

Beaufort Sea

National Petroleum
Reserve—Alaska

Point
Barrow *Plover Islands*
Barrow

Tangent Point
Point
Franklin   Cape Simpson
Peard Bay   *Smith   Pitt Point
Point Belcher   Bay*
Wainwright   Cape Halkett
Harrison Bay

William O. Douglas
Arctic Wildlife Range

Icy Cape   *Dease
Inlet*

*Teshekpuk
Lake*   Atigaru Point   *Simpson
Lagoon*   *Prudhoe
Bay*   *Mikkelsen Bay*

Point Lay   **Nuiqsut**   **Deadhorse** **Prudhoe
Bay**   Brownlow   Barter
Point   *Camden   Island*   **Kaktovik**
Bay

Cape Lisburne   **Wevok** Cape
Sabrine   Cape
Beaufort   Kavik   Demarcation
Point

Colville   River   North Slope—
Haul Road
(Dalton Highway)   Sadlerochit
Mountains   *Pulahula River*   British
Mountains

Point Hope   Noatak
National Monument   Trans-Alaska
Pipeline   Mount
Chamberlin
9,020   Romanzof
Mountains

Cape Thompson   B r o o k s   R a n g e

De Long Mountains   Endicott Mountains   *Lake*

Kivalina   Baird   Mountains   **Anaktuvuk
Pass**

Cape Krusenstern
National Monument   **Noatak**   Schwatka
Mountains

Cape Krusenstern   Gates of the Arctic
National Monument

Kotzebue   **Kiana**   *Kobuk*   **Ambler**
*Kotzebue   Baldwin   Waring   **Bornite**
Sound*   Peninsula   Mountains   *River*   **Kobuk**

Noorvik

*Selawik
Lake*   **Selawik**
Arctic Circle

Selawik National
Wildlife Refuge   Kobuk Valley
National Monument

Roads are indicated by red lines. All federal lands are
surrounded by black dotted lines. Federal lands include
National Forests, Monuments, Parks, Preserves and Wildlife
Refuges. With the exception of Selawik National Wildlife
Refuge, this map does not reflect boundary and name
changes resulting from the 1980 Alaska National Interest
Lands Conservation Act. (See index for new names.)

Scale
100 miles
100 kilometers

A
B
C
D
E
F
G

1 2 3 4 5 6 7 8 9 10 11 12

Left
The sheer, snow-covered
slopes of the Brooks Range
where it crosses the southern
portion of the Arctic National
Wildlife Refuge.
(Dennis and Debbie Miller)
Right
Light reflects off the braided
Hulahula River in the Arctic
National Wildlife Refuge.
(Dennis and Debbie Miller)

Above
Duck Island, a man-made island near Prudhoe Bay, on which Exxon has built a drilling rig.
(George Herben)

Left
Wildlife abounds on the waterways and tundra of the North Slope. Many species, such as this arctic loon family at Prudhoe Bay, will migrate out of the area in late summer to winter in more moderate climates.
(George Herben)

Right
Sohio Alaska Petroleum Company facilities at Prudhoe Bay. Sohio Alaska and ARCO Alaska are operators of the North Slope oil fields at Prudhoe Bay and Kuparuk.
(George Herben)

Left

Aerial view of Barrow, headquarters of the North Slope Borough and the commercial center of Alaska north of the Brooks Range. The airport, which serves Wien Air Alaska and several smaller charter services, extends diagonally across the top of the photo. The Top of the World Hotel is the inverted L-shaped building with the long pipe reaching to the surf. The three large buildings in the lower left are: North Slope Borough headquarters (blue roof); the store owned by the village corporation; and the Arctic Slope Regional Corporation headquarters (with orange stairway covering).
(Penny Rennick, Staff, reprinted from *ALASKA®* magazine)

Inupiat Eskimo whalers at Point Barrow search the ice leads (areas of open water which form when breakup comes) for signs of migrating bowheads.
(Alan Crane, reprinted from *ALASKA®* magazine)

Top
Frame for Ole and Manya Wik's semi-underground sod house in the Kobuk valley. The completed frame will be covered with plastic sheeting and moss, then backfilled with dirt. Additional insulation will be provided by snow.
(Manya Wik)

Above
Ole Wik takes the bedding out to air beside his semi-underground sod house.
(Manya Wik)

Above
On a foggy morning in the Kobuk valley, Keith Jones of Ambler hauls two sleds and a kayak by dog team to spring camp.
(Manya Wik)

Right
Eskimo women at Kobuk clean and hang fish on racks to dry. Fish is a staple in the diet of the Inupiat of the southwestern Arctic.
(William Sherwonit)

Below
Fishermen gather to sell their chum salmon to a buyer at Kotzebue, site of the farthest north commercial fishery.
(Bruce Baker, reprinted from *ALASKA*® magazine)

Right
NANA, the Native regional corporation for the Kotzebue area, manages the largest reindeer herd in Alaska. About 6,000 animals graze on the Baldwin Peninsula (on which Kotzebue is situated). During the summer the antlers are cut from the reindeer and sold to processors who grind the antlers into a compound for resale in the Orient.
(George Herben)

The changing seasons at Kotzebue: July (below) and March (right). In summer commerce, tourism, commercial fishing and subsistence support the town's 2,250 residents. In winter trapping becomes a source of revenue. Kotzebue boasts a radio station, cable TV and two fine museums.
(Both by George Herben)

ALASKA

Appendix

Portions of the following are excerpted from *The MILEPOST* ® (1983 edition) available for $11.95 (plus $1.00 fourth class or $3.00 first class postage and handling), and *THE ALASKA ALMANAC*® (1983 edition) available for $4.95 (plus $1.00 postage and handling); both from Alaska Northwest Publishing Company, Box 4-EEE, Anchorage, Alaska 99509.

OPPOSITE: Alaska's plants and wildlife, painted by the late Bill Berry, one of Alaska's leading artists for many years. The 26½-inch-by-40-inch map, detailing 120 flowers, animals, fishes and birds, is available for $6.00 (plus $1.00 postage and handling) from Alaska Northwest Publishing, Box 4-EEE, Anchorage, Alaska 99509. Maps come in a protective tube and with a numbered key identifying each species.

PHYSICAL GEOGRAPHY OF ALASKA

LAND

At first glance it seems impossible that such a huge country as Alaska has not been more widely settled. Thousands of acres of forest and tundra, miles and miles of rivers and streams, hidden valleys, bays, coves and mountains, are spread across an area so vast that it staggers the imagination. Yet, nearly two-thirds of the population of Alaska remains clustered around two major centers of commerce and survival. Compared to the settlement of the West, Alaska is not settled at all.

Visitors flying over the state are always impressed by the immense areas with no sign of humanity. Current assessments indicate that approximately 160,000 acres of Alaska have been cleared, built on or otherwise directly altered by man, either by settlement or resource development, including mining, pipeline construction, and agriculture. In comparison to the 375 million acres of land which comprise the state, the settled or altered area currently amounts to less than 1/20th of a percent.

There are significant reasons for this lack of development in Alaska. Frozen for long periods in the dark of the Arctic, much of the land cannot support quantities of people or industry and where the winters are warmer, the mountains, glaciers, rivers and oceans prevent easy access for commerce and trade.

The status of land, especially in Alaska, is constantly changing. In most places, the free market affects patterns of land ownership, but in Alaska, all land ownership patterns until recently were the result of a century-long process of a single landowner, the United States government.

The Statehood Act signaled the beginning of a dramatic shift in land ownership. It authorized the state to select a total of 104 million of the 375 million acres of land and inland waters in Alaska. Under the Submerged Lands Act, the state also has title to submerged lands under navigable inland waters. In passing the Statehood Act, Congress cited economic independence and the need to open Alaska to economic development as the primary purposes for large state land grants.

The issue of the Native claims in Alaska was cleared with the passage of the Alaska Native Claims Settlement Act (ANCSA) on December 18, 1971. This act of Congress provided for creation of Alaska Native village and regional corporations, and gave the Alaska Eskimos, Aleuts and Indians nearly $1 billion and the right to select 44 million acres from a land "pool" of some 116 million acres.

Immediately after the passage of the ANCSA, the state filed for the selection of an additional 77 million acres of land before the creation of some Native withdrawals and withdrawals for study as "National Interest

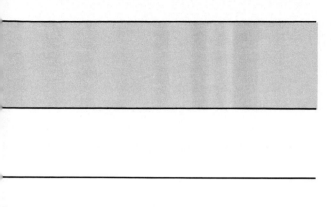

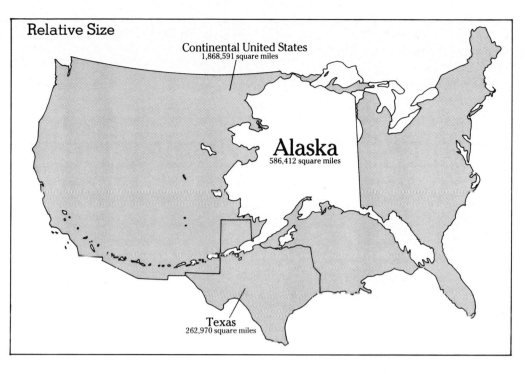

Relative Size

Continental United States
1,868,591 square miles

Alaska
586,412 square miles

Texas
262,970 square miles

Lands." The Department of the Interior refused to recognize these selections. In September 1972 the litigation initiated by the state was resolved by a settlement affirming state selection of 41 million acres.

Section 17 of ANCSA, in addition to establishing a Joint Federal-State Land Use Planning Commission, directed the Secretary of the Interior to withdraw from public use up to 80 million acres of land in Alaska for study as possible national parks, wildlife refuges, forests, and wild and scenic rivers. These were the "National Interest Lands" Congress was to decide upon as set forth in subsection 17(d)(2) of the act, by December 18, 1978. The U.S. House of Representatives passed a bill (HR39) which would have designated 124 million acres of national parks, forests and wildlife refuges, and designated millions of acres of these and existing parks, forests and refuges as wilderness. Although a bill was reported out of Committee, it failed to pass the Senate before Congress adjourned.

In November 1978 the Secretary of the Interior published a draft environmental impact statement which listed the options that the executive branch of the federal government had to protect federal lands in Alaska until the 96th Congress could consider the creation of new parks, wildlife refuges, wild and scenic rivers and forests. In keeping with this objective, the Secretary of the Interior withdrew from most public uses about 114 million acres of land in Alaska, under provisions of the 1976 Federal Land Policy and Management Act. On December 1, 1978, the president, under the authority of the 1906 Antiquities Act, designated 56 million acres of these lands as national monuments.

In February 1980 the House of Representatives passed a modified HR39. In August 1980 the Senate passed a compromise version of the Alaska lands bill which created 106 million acres of new conservation units and affected a total of 131 million acres of land in Alaska. In November 1980 the House accepted the Senate version of the Alaska National Interest Lands Conservation Act, which President Jimmy Carter signed into law on December 2, 1980. This is also known as the d-2 lands bill or the compromise HR39.

Alaska's land will continue to be a controversial and complex subject for some time. Resolution of the d-2 issue, and distribution of land to Native village and regional corporations, the state of Alaska, and private citizens in the state will require time. Numerous land issues created by large land exchanges, conflicting land use and management policies, and overlapping resources will require constant cooperation between landowners if the issues are going to be solved successfully.

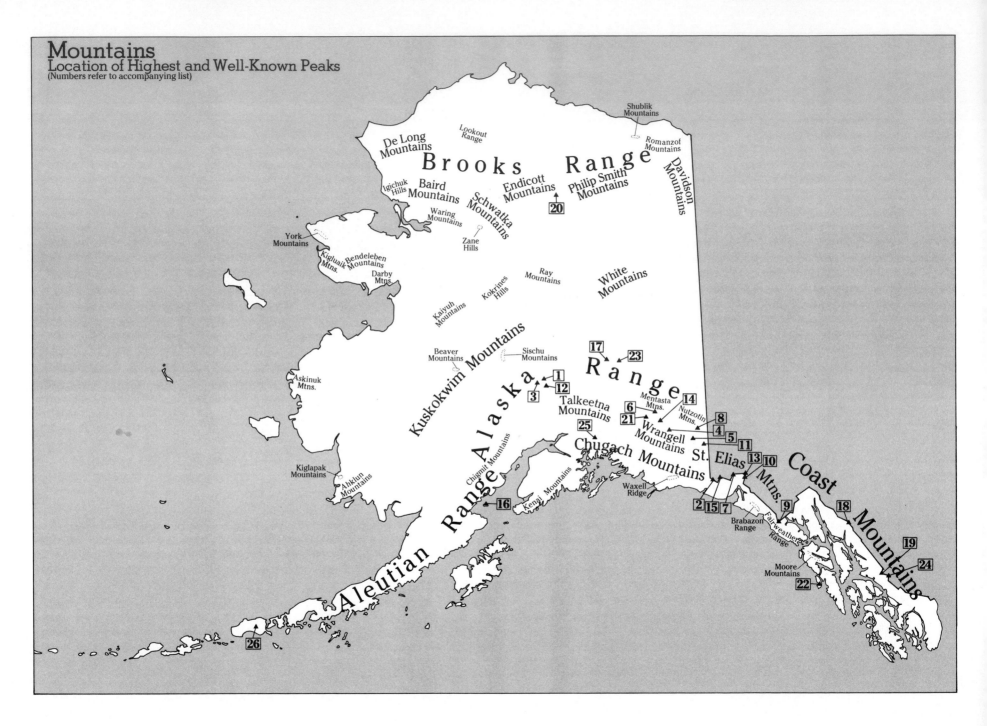

Mountains
Location of Highest and Well-Known Peaks
(Numbers refer to accompanying list)

Shublik Mountains

Lookout Range

De Long Mountains

Romanzof Mountains

Brooks   Range

Davidson Mountains

Igichuk Hills

Baird Mountains

Endicott Mountains

Philip Smith Mountains

Schwatka Mountains

[20]

Waring Mountains

York Mountains

Zane Hills

Kigluaik Mtns.

Bendeleben Mountains

Darby Mtns.

Ray Mountains

White Mountains

Kaiyuh Mountains

Kokrines Hills

Beaver Mountains

Sischu Mountains

[17] [23]

Kuskokwim Mountains

Range

Askinuk Mtns.

[1]
[12]
[3]

Mentasta Mtns.

[14]

Talkeetna Mountains

Alaska

Nutzotin Mtns.

[6]
[21]

[8]

Wrangell Mountains

[4]
[5]

Kiglapak Mountains

Ahklun Mountains

[25]

Chugach Mountains

St. Elias

[11]
[13] [10]

Mtns.

Coast

Chigmit Mountains

Kenai Mountains

Waxell Ridge

[2] [15] [7]

[9]

[18]

Mountains

[16]

Brabazon Range

Fairweather Range

[19]

Aleutian   Range

Moore Mountains

[22]

[24]

[26]

132

MOUNTAINS

Of the 20 highest mountains in the United States, 17 are in Alaska, which has 19 peaks over 14,000 feet. The U.S. Geological Survey lists them as follows:

Highest Mountains

MAP KEY	ELEVATION
1 McKinley, South Peak	20,320
1 McKinley, North Peak	19,470
2 Saint Elias*	18,008
3 Foraker	17,400
4 Blackburn	16,523
5 Bona	16,421
6 Sanford	16,237
1 South Buttress	15,885
7 Vancouver*	15,700
8 Churchill	15,638

MAP KEY	ELEVATION
9 Fairweather*	15,300
10 Hubbard*	15,015
11 Bear	14,831
1 East Buttress	14,730
12 Hunter	14,573
13 Alverstone*	14,565
1 Browne Tower	14,530
14 Wrangell	14,163
15 Augusta*	14,070

*On Alaska-Canada border.

Other Well-Known Alaska Mountains

MAP KEY	ELEVATION
16 Augustine Volcano	4,025
17 Deborah	12,339
18 Devils Paw	8,584
19 Devils Thumb	9,077
20 Doonerak	7,610
21 Drum	12,010
22 Edgecumbe	3,201
23 Hayes	13,832
24 Kates Needle	10,002
25 Marcus Baker	13,176
26 Shishaldin	9,372

Mountain Ranges

	ELEVATION
Ahklun Mountains	1,000-3,000
Alaska Range	to 20,320
Aleutian Range	to 7,585
Askinuk Mountains	to 2,342
Baird Mountains	to 4,300
Bendeleben Mountains	to 3,730
Brabazon Range	to 5,515
Brooks Range	4,000-9,000
Chigmit Mountains	to 5,000
Chugach Mountains	to 13,176
Coast Mountains	to 18,000
Darby Mountains	to 3,083
Davidson Mountains	to 5,540

	ELEVATION
De Long Mountains	to 4,886
Endicott Mountains	to 7,000
Fairweather Range	to 15,300
Igichuk Hills	to 2,000
Kaiyuh Mountains	1,000-2,844
Kenai Mountains	to 6,000
Kiglapak Mountains	to 1,070
Kigluaik Mountains	to 4,714
Kuskokwim Mountains	to 3,973
Lookout Range	to 2,400
Mentasta Mountains	4,000-7,000
Moore Mountains	to 3,000
Nutzotin Mountains	5,000-8,000

	ELEVATION
Ray Mountains	2,500-5,500
Romanzof Mountains	to 8,700
Saint Elias Mountains	to 18,000
Schwatka Mountains	to 8,800
Shublik Mountains	to 4,500
Sischu Mountains	to 2,422
Talkeetna Mountains	6,000-8,800
Waring Mountains	to 1,800
Waxell Ridge	4,000-10,000
White Mountains	to 5,000
Wrangell Mountains	to 16,421
York Mountains	to 2,349
Zane Hills	to 4,053

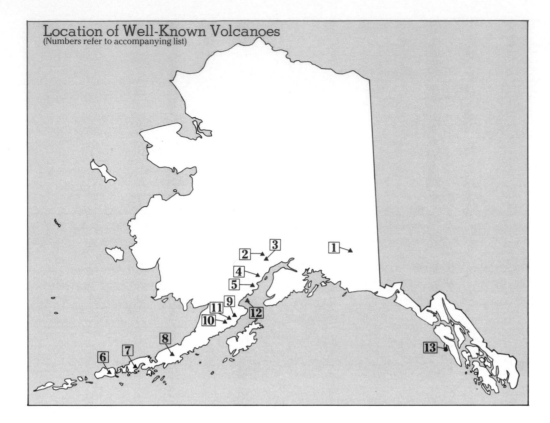

Location of Well-Known Volcanoes
(Numbers refer to accompanying list)

VOLCANOES

The state's 10 tallest volcanic peaks, as listed by the National Geographic Society, are as follows:

MAP KEY	ELEVATION
1 Mount Wrangell	14,163
2 Mount Torbert	11,413
3 Mount Spurr	11,069
4 Redoubt Volcano	10,197
5 Iliamna Volcano	10,016
6 Shishaldin Volcano	9,387
7 Pavlof Volcano	8,261
8 Mount Veniaminof	8,225
9 Mount Griggs	7,600
10 Mount Mageik	7,250

Other Volcanic Peaks

MAP KEY	ELEVATION
11 Mount Katmai	6,715
12 Augustine Volcano	4,025
13 Mount Edgecumbe	3,201

The Aleutian Islands and the Alaska Peninsula are part of the "rim of fire" that surrounds the Pacific basin. The majority of the region's 57 volcanic mountains have been active since 1760. The major eruption in modern times was the Mount Katmai eruption of 1912. On November 11, 1980, Pavlof Volcano, on the lower Alaska Peninsula 35 miles northeast of Cold Bay, erupted for the first time since 1976, sending plumes of steam and ash 20,000 feet in the air. Pavlof has had a long history of eruptions; more than 25 separate eruptions since 1700.

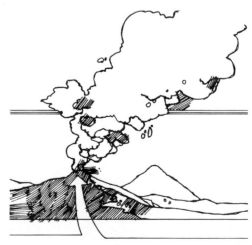

RIVERS

Following are the 10 longest rivers in Alaska, according to the Army Corps of Engineers:

MAP KEY	MILES
1 Yukon*	1,875
2 Porcupine**	555
3 Koyukuk	554
4 Kuskokwim	540
5 Tanana	531
6 Innoko	463
7 Colville	428
8 Noatak	396
9 Kobuk	347
10 Birch Creek	314

*The Yukon flows about 1,400 miles in Alaska; the remainder is in Canada. It ranks fourth in North America in length, fifth in drainage area (327,600 square miles).
**About two-thirds of the Porcupine's length is in Canada.

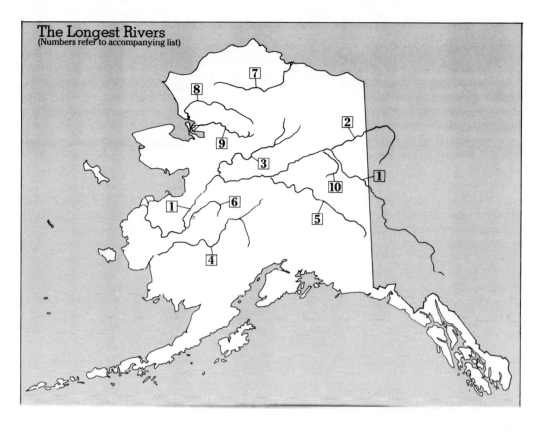

The Longest Rivers
(Numbers refer to accompanying list)

LAKES

There are 94 lakes with surface areas of more than 10 square miles among Alaska's more than 3 million lakes. According to a 1963 report of the U.S. Geological Survey, the 10 largest natural freshwater lakes are:

	SQUARE MILES
Iliamna	1,000
Becharof	458
Teshekpuk	315
Naknek	242
Tustumena	117
Clark	110
Dall	100
Upper Ugashik	75
Lower Ugashik	72
Kukaklek	72

ISLANDS

Southeastern Alaska contains about 1,000 of the state's 1,800 named islands, rocks and reefs; several thousand remain unnamed. There are more than 200 islands in the Aleutian Island chain in southwestern Alaska. Of the state's 10 largest islands, six are in southeastern Alaska. Of the remainder, Unimak is in the Aleutians, Nunivak and Saint Lawrence are in the Bering Sea off the west coast of Alaska, and Kodiak is in the Gulf of Alaska. The state's 10 largest islands, according to U.S. Geological Survey and Bureau of Land Management figures, are:

	SQUARE MILES
Kodiak	3,588
Prince of Wales	2,231
Chichagof	2,062
Saint Lawrence	1,780*
Admiralty	1,709
Baranof	1,636
Nunivak	1,600*
Unimak	1,600
Revillagigedo	1,134
Kupreanof	1,084

*Estimate

135

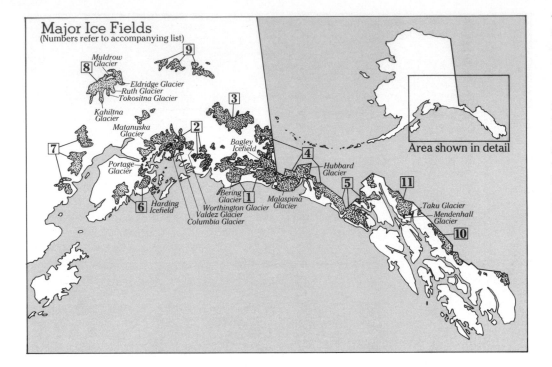

Major Ice Fields
(Numbers refer to accompanying list)

GLACIERS AND ICE FIELDS

The greatest concentrations of glaciers are in the Alaska Range, Wrangell Mountains, and the coastal ranges of the Chugach, Coast, Kenai and Saint Elias mountains, where annual precipitation is high. All of Alaska's well-known glaciers fall within these massive ice fields. The accompanying map shows the most extensive ice coverage according to the U.S. Geological Survey.

Glaciers cover approximately 29,000 square miles—or 4.9 percent—of Alaska. There are an estimated 100,000 glaciers in Alaska, ranging from tiny cirque glaciers to huge valley glaciers.

Alaska's glaciers fall into roughly five general categories: alpine, valley, piedmont, ice fields and icecaps. Alpine (mountain and cirque) glaciers head high on the slopes of mountains and plateaus. Valley glaciers are an overflowing accumulation of ice from mountain or plateau basins. Piedmont glaciers form when one or more valley glaciers meet at the base of a slope, flowing into a fan-shaped ice mass (called a piedmont lobe) at the foot of a mountain range. Ice fields develop when large valley glaciers interconnect, separated by mountain peaks. Icecaps are snow- and ice-filled basins or plateaus.

Alaska's better-known glaciers accessible by road are: Worthington and Black Rapids (Richardson Highway); Matanuska (Glenn Highway); Portage (Seward Highway); and Mendenhall (Glacier Highway). In addition, Childs and Sheridan glaciers may be reached by car from Cordova, and Valdez Glacier is only a few miles from the town of Valdez. The sediment-covered terminus of Muldrow Glacier in Denali National Park and Preserve is visible at a distance for several miles from the park road.

Many spectacular glaciers in Glacier Bay National Park and Preserve and in Prince William Sound are accessible by tour boat.

MAP KEY	SQUARE MILES
1 Chugach Mountains (eastern) includes Bagley Icefield, Bering, Childs, Miles and Sheridan glaciers	4,700
2 Chugach Mountains (central and western) includes Blackstone, Columbia, Knik, Matanuska, Portage, Twentymile, and Worthington glaciers and Sargent Icefield	3,550
3 Wrangell Mountains includes Chisana, Kennicott and Nabesna glaciers	3,200
4 Saint Elias Mountains (Yakutat Bay area) includes Agassiz, Hubbard, Malaspina and Seward glaciers	2,900
5 Saint Elias Mountains (Glacier Bay and Fairweather Range) includes Brady and La Perouse glaciers and 13 active tidewater glaciers	2,600
6 Kenai Mountains includes Harding Icefield	1,850
7 Alaska Range (southwestern) includes Hayes and Capps glaciers	1,850
8 Alaska Range (Mount McKinley area) includes Kahiltna, Muldrow, Ruth, Yentna-Lacuna, Eldridge and Tokositna glaciers	1,750
9 Alaska Range (eastern) includes Black Rapids, Canwell, Castner, Gulkana, Johnson and Susitna glaciers	1,450
10 Coast Mountains (Stikine Icefield) includes LeConte Glacier	1,300
11 Coast Mountains (Juneau Icefield) includes Mendenhall and Taku glaciers	1,200
TOTAL	26,350

CLIMATE

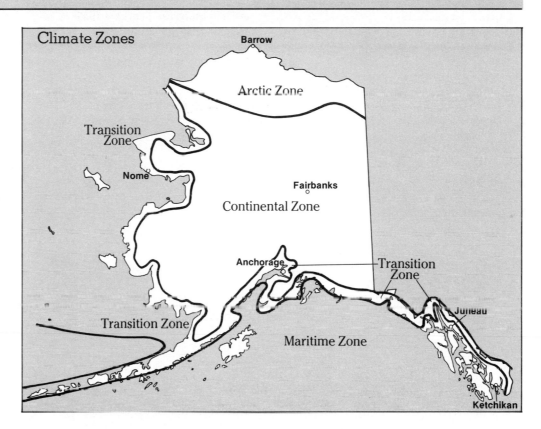

Climate Zones

Barrow

Arctic Zone

Transition Zone

Nome

Fairbanks

Continental Zone

Anchorage

Transition Zone

Transition Zone

Juneau

Maritime Zone

Ketchikan

Alaska's climate zones are maritime, transition, continental and arctic (see map, right).

Maritime includes Southeast, the Aleutian Chain and the immediate coastal area of the Gulf Coast. Temperatures are comparatively mild, and precipitation—mostly rain—is heavy, from 50 to 200 inches annually along the coast and up to 400 inches on the mountain slopes.

The Aleutians maintain a reputation as the windiest area in Alaska, with Amchitka being the windiest weather recording station in the state, followed by Cold Bay.

The roughest seas occur in the Gulf of Alaska. Waves up to 43 feet high have been reported south of Kodiak in midwinter, and waves of 50 feet in height south of Yakutat.

Transition, between maritime and continental, lies between the Coast Mountains and the Alaska Range and includes Anchorage and the Matanuska Valley, as well as the Bering Sea coast, which is too severe to be maritime but is milder than the Interior or Arctic. Summer temperatures are higher than the maritime climate, winter temperatures lower and precipitation less.

Continental covers the majority of the body of Alaska except the coastal fringes and arctic slope. It has extreme high and low temperatures and light precipitation.

Arctic, north of the Brooks Range, has cold winters, cool summers and desertlike precipitation. The arctic ice pack usually descends on shore in early October and retreats in mid-July to late August.

CLIMATE RECORDS

Highest temperature: 100° F, at Fort Yukon, June 27, 1915.

Lowest temperature: -80° F, at Prospect Creek Camp, January 23, 1971.

Most annual average precipitation: 332.29 inches, at MacLeod Harbor (Montague Island), 1976.

Most precipitation in 24 hours: 14.84 inches, in Little Port Walter, December 6, 1964.

Least precipitation in a year: 1.61 inches, at Barrow, 1935.

Most monthly precipitation: 70.99 inches, at MacLeod Harbor, November 1976.

Most snowfall in a season: 974.5 inches, at Thompson Pass, 1952-53.

Most snowfall in 24 hours: 62 inches, at Thompson Pass, December 1955.

Most monthly snowfall: 297.9 inches, at Thompson Pass, February 1953.

Least snowfall in a season: 3 inches, at Barrow, 1935-36.

Highest recorded snow depth in one season (also highest ever recorded in North America): 356 inches on Wolverine Glacier, Kenai Peninsula, after winter of 1976-77.

Highest recorded wind speed: 139 mph, at Shemya Island, December 1959.

CHILL FACTOR

Wind chill can lower the effective temperature many degrees. While Alaska's regions of lowest temperatures also generally have little wind, activity such as riding a snowmobile or even walking can produce the same effect on exposed skin.

TEMPERATURE (FAHRENHEIT)	EFFECTIVE TEMPERATURE WITH WIND SPEED OF . . .		
	10 mph	20 mph	30 mph
40	28	18	13
30	16	4	-2
20	4	-10	-18
10	-9	-25	-33
0	-21	-39	-48
-10	-33	-53	-63
-20	-46	-67	-79
-30	-58	-82	-94
-40	-70	-96	-109

PERMAFROST

Permanently frozen subsoil, continuous in polar regions, underlies the entire arctic region to depths reported to reach 2,000 feet. Permafrost influences construction in the Arctic because building on it causes thawing and therefore heaving of the melted ground.

Much of the Interior and some of South-central are underlain by discontinuous permafrost. Permafrost is responsible for the thousands of lakes dotting the arctic tundra because ground water is held on the surface.

	Anchorage	Barrow	Bethel	Cold Bay	Fairbanks	Homer	Juneau	Ketchikan	King Salmon	Kodiak	McGrath	Nome	Petersburg	Valdez
January														
Temperature	11.8	-14.7	5.1	28.2	-11.9	21.4	23.5	33.0	13.4	30.4	-8.9	6.0	25.3	17.8
Precipitation	0.84	0.23	0.54	2.42	0.60	1.70	3.94	14.49	0.94	5.01	0.85	0.90	8.83	5.06
February														
Temperature	17.8	-18.6	8.2	28.2	-2.5	24.9	28.0	37.0	16.6	31.4	-.2	5.2	30.8	22.4
Precipitation	0.84	0.20	0.74	2.59	0.53	1.54	3.44	14.08	0.99	4.89	0.90	0.84	8.59	5.30
March														
Temperature	23.7	-15.2	11.4	29.0	9.5	27.6	31.9	38.2	20.4	32.1	8.9	7.4	33.6	26.8
Precipitation	0.56	0.19	0.79	1.93	0.48	1.22	3.57	11.90	1.16	3.85	0.86	0.79	6.87	4.33
April														
Temperature	35.3	-.9	24.5	33.1	28.9	35.0	38.9	43.0	31.5	36.9	26.5	18.9	39.7	35.6
Precipitation	0.56	0.21	0.43	1.54	0.33	1.09	2.99	12.60	0.90	3.81	0.66	0.73	7.11	3.06
May														
Temperature	46.2	19.1	40.1	39.5	47.3	42.3	46.8	49.2	42.6	43.2	44.1	34.8	46.6	43.8
Precipitation	0.59	0.17	0.83	2.19	0.65	0.91	3.31	9.69	1.13	4.35	0.80	0.70	6.05	3.20
June														
Temperature	54.6	33.0	51.6	45.4	59.0	48.7	53.2	54.1	50.7	49.7	55.7	45.5	52.4	51.2
Precipitation	1.07	0.35	1.24	1.84	1.42	1.06	2.93	7.80	1.44	4.12	1.70	0.95	5.32	2.70
July														
Temperature	57.9	38.7	54.7	50.1	60.7	52.3	55.7	58.2	54.5	54.1	58.2	50.1	55.8	53.3
Precipitation	2.07	0.88	1.98	2.22	1.90	1.70	4.69	7.81	2.18	3.54	2.28	2.42	5.26	4.31
August														
Temperature	55.9	37.6	52.3	51.3	55.4	52.4	54.3	58.3	53.8	54.9	53.5	49.2	54.7	52.0
Precipitation	2.32	1.04	3.97	3.89	2.19	2.56	5.00	12.09	3.46	4.30	3.28	3.57	7.54	5.80
September														
Temperature	48.1	30.3	45.0	47.3	44.4	47.0	49.2	54.1	47.3	50.0	43.8	42.1	49.9	46.5
Precipitation	2.37	0.58	2.42	3.95	1.08	2.85	6.90	13.86	3.07	6.11	2.14	2.40	10.73	7.74
October														
Temperature	34.8	15.3	30.2	39.6	25.2	37.4	41.8	46.6	33.6	40.7	25.3	28.5	42.8	37.5
Precipitation	1.43	0.55	1.32	4.31	0.73	3.38	7.85	25.03	2.00	6.29	1.22	1.42	16.57	6.75
November														
Temperature	21.1	-.5	17.2	34.3	2.8	28.2	32.5	39.8	22.1	34.8	5.0	15.6	35.0	26.1
Precipitation	1.02	0.30	0.96	3.90	0.66	2.76	5.53	17.08	1.43	5.41	1.03	0.98	11.2	5.67
December														
Temperature	13.0	-12.3	4.4	29.0	-10.4	21.4	27.3	36.2	11.7	29.9	-9.2	4.4	30.1	19.5
Precipitation	1.07	0.19	0.62	2.45	0.65	2.29	4.52	17.22	1.05	5.03	1.02	0.74	11.18	5.39
Snowfall (max)	41.6	9.7	17.6	24.2	33.5	44.2	54.7	39.0	16.0	33.1	50.9	23.4	25.5	101.5

TOWNS AND VILLAGES

Alaska's 400,000-plus residents are distributed among more than 330 towns and villages from Ketchikan to Barrow—with more than half in the Anchorage trading area. Three-fourths of the state's residents live in the 14 communities with a population over 2,000—the remainder are largely in villages with fewer than 500 people. The vast majority of Alaska's towns and villages are along seacoasts or rivers. Relatively few are connected to the state's modest highway system.

CENSUS AREAS

Most states are divided into counties. In Alaska, which has no counties, the equivalent are organized boroughs and "census areas." Census areas were developed for general statistical purposes by the state of Alaska and Census Bureau. Census areas and populations shown here are from the U.S. Department of Commerce 1980 *Census of Population*.

CENSUS AREA CODES	CENSUS AREA	1980 POPULATION
	Alaska	401,851
13	Municipality of Anchorage	174,431
05	Fairbanks-North Star Borough	53,983
14	Kenai Peninsula Borough	25,282
19	City & Borough of Juneau	19,528
12	Matanuska Susitna Borough	17,816
23	Ketchikan Gateway Borough	11,316
08	Bethel	10,999
15	Kodiak Island Borough	9,939
16	Valdez-Cordova	8,348
04	Yukon-Koyukuk	7,873
20	Sitka City & Borough	7,803
11	Aleutian Islands	7,768
03	Nome	6,537
21	Wrangell-Petersburg	6,167
06	Southeast Fairbanks	5,676
02	Kobuk	4,831
07	Wade Hampton	4,665
09	Dillingham	4,616
01	North Slope Borough	4,199
22	Prince of Wales-Outer Ketchikan	3,822
17	Skagway-Yakutat-Angoon	3,478
18	Haines Borough	1,680
10	Bristol Bay Borough	1,094

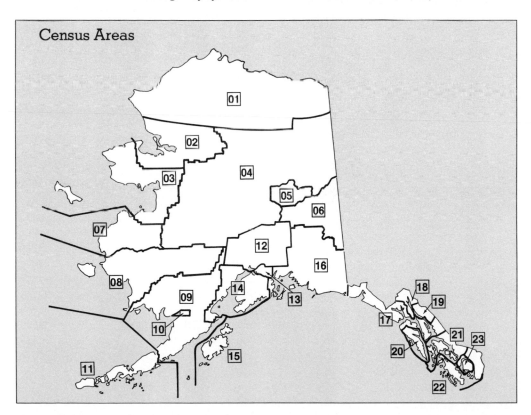

Census Areas

Age and Gender of Alaskans

Median age about 26
Men: 53% of population
Women: 47% of population

Alaskans by Age, 1970 and 1980

- - - - 1970 Total 302,361
———— 1980 Total 400,481

Age

Source: U.S. census data compiled by the
Alaska Department of Labor

Births and Deaths

According to the Alaska Department of
Health and Social Services, in 1980 there were
9,463 births, 1,730 deaths, 5,385 marriages,
3,533 divorces and 647 adoptions.

POPULATIONS AND ZIP CODES

Alaska's population at the time of the 1980 census was 401,851. A July 1981 estimate by the Alaska Department of Labor placed the state's population at 422,187. The populations for cities and communities in the following list are taken from both the U.S. Department of Commerce 1980 *Census of Population* and the Alaska Department of Labor 1981 *Alaska Population Overview.* Population figures for communities designated CDP (Census Designated Places) are taken from the 1980 census. Populations for incorporated cities (followed by the date of incorporation) are taken from the 1981 Department of Labor estimate. The abbreviation NA indicates population figures are not available and/or zip codes are not available.

COMMUNITY	POPULATION	ZIP CODE
Adak (CDP)	3,315	99695
Akhiok (1972)	103	99615
Akiachak (1974)	435	99551
Akiak (1970)	197	99552
Akolmiut (1969)	695	99695
Akutan (1979)	189	99553
Alakanuk (1969)	534	99554
Aleknagik (1973)	152	99555
Alitak	NA	99615
Allakaket (1975)	158	99720
Ambler (1971)	198	99786
Amchitka Island	NA	99541
Anaktuvuk Pass (1957)	235	99721
Anchorage (municipality)	180,740	995 --
Anchor Point (CDP)	226	99556
Anderson (1962)	500	99790
Angoon (1963)	445	99820
Aniak (1972)	338	99557
Annette (CDP)	139	99920
Anvik (1969)	110	99558
Arctic Village (CDP)	111	99722
Atka (CDP)	93	99502
Atkasook (CDP)	107	NA
Atmautluak (1976)	226	99559
Attu (CDP)	29	99502
Auke Bay	NA	99821
Baranof	NA	99833
Barrow (1959)	2,539	99723
Beaver (CDP)	66	99724
Belkofski	NA	99695
Bethel (1957)	3,549	99559
Big Delta (CDP)	285	99737
Big Horn (CDP)	360	NA
Big Lake (CDP)	410	99695
Big Mountain	NA	99695

COMMUNITY	POPULATION	ZIP CODE
Birch Creek (CDP)	32	99790
Birchwood	NA	99501
Bodenburg Butte (CDP)	988	NA
Boundary	NA	99790
Brevig Mission (1969)	149	99785
Buckland (1966)	211	99727
Campion Station (CDP)	62	NA
Candle	NA	NA
Cantwell (CDP)	89	99729
Cape Lisburne (CDP)	36	99790
Cape Newenham (CDP)	43	99695
Cape Pole (CDP)	29	NA
Cape Sarichef	NA	99695
Cape Yakataga	NA	99560
Central (CDP)	36	99730
Chalkyitsik (CDP)	100	99788
Chatanika	NA	99731
Chefornak (1974)	230	99561
Chevak (1967)	491	99563
Chicken (CDP)	37	99732
Chignik (CDP)	178	99564
Chignik Lagoon (CDP)	48	99565
Chignik Lake (CDP)	138	99695
Chistochina (CDP)	55	99586
Chitina (CDP)	42	99566
Chuathbaluk	104	99557
Chugiak	NA	99567
Circle (CDP)	81	99733
Clam Gulch (CDP)	50	99568
Clarks Point (1971)	78	99569
Clear	NA	99704
Clover Pass (CDP)	451	NA
Coffman Cove (CDP)	193	NA
Cohoe	NA	99669
Cold Bay (1982)	228	99571

COMMUNITY	POPULATION	ZIP CODE
College (CDP)	4,043	99701
Cooper Landing (CDP)	116	99572
Copper Center (CDP)	213	99573
Cordova (1909)	2,223	99574
Craig (1922)	560	99921
Crooked Creek (CDP)	108	99575
Deering (1970)	155	99736
Delta Junction (1960)	945	99737
Denali Nat'l. Park (CDP) formerly McKinley Park	32	99755
Dillingham (1963)	1,670	99576
Diomede (1970)	149	NA
Dot Lake (CDP)	67	99737
Douglas	NA	99824
Dutch Harbor	NA	99692
Eagle (1901)	186	99738
Eagle River	NA	99577
Edna Bay	NA	99950
Eek (1970)	226	99578
Egegik (CDP)	75	99579
Eielson Air Force Base (CDP)	5,232	99702
Eklutna	NA	99790
Ekuk	NA	99695
Ekwok (1974)	76	99580
Elfin Cove (CDP)	28	99825
Elim (1970)	228	99739
Elmendorf Air Force Base	NA	99506
Emmonak (1964)	568	99581
English Bay (CDP)	124	99695
Ester (CDP)	149	99725
Evansville (CDP)	94	99726
Excursion Inlet	NA	99850
Fairbanks (city)	25,568	99701
False Pass (CDP)	70	99583
Fire Lake	475	99695
Flat	NA	99584

COMMUNITY	POPULATION	ZIP CODE
Fort Greely (CDP)	1,635	99790
Fort Richardson	NA	99505
Fortuna Ledge (1970)	243	99585
Fort Wainwright	NA	99703
Fort Yukon (1959)	599	99740
Fox (CDP)	123	99790
Fritz Creek (CDP)	302	99697
Gakona (CDP)	87	99586
Galena (1971)	805	99741
Gambell (1963)	480	99742
Girdwood	NA	99587
Glennallen (CDP)	511	99588
Golovin (1971)	94	99762
Goodnews Bay (1970)	167	99589
Graehl	NA	99701
Granite Mountain	NA	99790
Grayling (1969)	202	99590
Gulkana (CDP)	104	99695
Gustavus (CDP)	98	99826
Haines (1910)	1,017	99827
Halibut Cove (CDP)	47	99603
Healy (CDP)	334	99743
Herring Cove (CDP)	99	NA
Holy Cross (1968)	233	99602
Homer (1964)	2,588	99603
Hoonah (1946)	799	99829
Hooper Bay (1966)	624	99604
Hope (CDP)	103	99605
Houston (1966)	583	99697
Hughes (1973)	71	99745
Huslia (1969)	230	99746
Hydaburg (1927)	356	99922
Hyder (CDP)	77	99923
Igiugig (CDP)	33	99695
Iliamna (CDP)	94	99606

COMMUNITY	POPULATION	ZIP CODE
Indian Mountain (CDP)	27APO	98748
Ivanof Bay (CDP)	40	99695
Jakolof Bay (CDP)	36	NA
Juneau (city and borough)	21,080	99801
Kachemak (1961)	425	NA
Kaguyak	NA	99697
Kake (1952)	583	99830
Kaktovik (1971)	201	99747
Kalifonsky (CDP)	92	NA
Kalskag	NA	99607
Kaltag (1969)	239	99748
Karluk (CDP)	96	99608
Kasaan (1976)	64	NA
Kasilof (CDP)	201	99610
Kenai (1960)	4,558	99611
Ketchikan (1900)	7,200	99901
Kiana (1964)	356	99749
King Cove (1947)	513	99612
King Salmon (CDP)	545	99613
Kipnuk (CDP)	371	99614
Kivalina (1969)	249	99750
Klawock (1929)	389	99925
Klukwan (CDP)	135	NA
Kobuk (1973)	64	99751
Kodiak (1940)	4,678	99615
Kodiak Naval Station (CDP)	1,370	NA
Kokhanok (CDP)	83	99606
Koliganek (CDP)	117	99576
Kongiganak (CDP)	239	99559
Kotlik (1970)	339	99620
Kotzebue (1958)	2,250	99752
Koyuk (1970)	203	99753
Koyukuk (1973)	95	99754

COMMUNITY	POPULATION	ZIP CODE
Kupreanof (1975)	49	NA
Kwethluk (1975)	451	99621
Kwigillingok (CDP)	354	99622
Lake Minchumina	NA	99623
Larsen Bay (1974)	167	99624
Levelock (CDP)	79	99625
Lime Village (CDP)	48	99695
Little Diomede Village	NA	99762
Livengood	NA	99790
Lower Kalskag (1969)	244	99626
Lower Tonsina (CDP)	40	NA
Manley Hot Springs (CDP)	61	99756
Manokotak (1970)	290	99628
Marshall	NA	99585
McGrath (1975)	343	99627
Medfra	NA	99629
Mekoryuk (1969)	176	99630
Mentasta Lake (CDP)	59	99695
Metlakatla (CDP)	1,056	99926
Meyers Chuck (CDP)	50	99903
Minto (CDP)	153	99758
Montana (CDP)	40	99695
Moose Creek (CDP)	510	99674
Moose Pass (CDP)	76	99631
Moser Bay	NA	99697
Mountain Point (CDP)	396	NA
Mountain View	NA	99504
Mountain Village (1967)	580	99632
Murphy Dome (CDP)	72	99790
Naknek (CDP)	318	99633
Napakiak (1970)	283	99634
Napaskiak (1971)	242	99559
Nelson Lagoon (CDP)	59	99697
Nenana (1921)	592	99760
Newhalen (1971)	135	NA

COMMUNITY	POPULATION	ZIP CODE
New Stuyahok (1972)	327	99636
Newtok (1976)	175	99559
Nightmute (1974)	135	99690
Nikishka (CDP) A.k.a. Port Nikiski	1,109	99611
Nikolai (1970)	88	99691
Nikolski (CDP)	50	99638
Ninilchik (CDP)	341	99639
Noatak (CDP)	273	99761
Nome (1901)	3,039	99762
Nondalton (1971)	171	99640
Noorvik (1964)	508	99763
North Pole (1953)	928	99705
North Whale Pass (CDP)	90	NA
Northway (CDP)	73	99764
Northway Village (CDP)	112	NA
Nuiqsut (1975)	270	NA
Nulato (1963)	338	99765
Old Harbor (1966)	334	99643
Oscarville (CDP)	56	99695
Ouzinkie (1967)	170	99644
Palmer (1951)	2,275	99645
Paxson (CDP)	30	99737
Pedro Bay (CDP)	33	99647
Pelican (1943)	172	99832
Pennock Island (CDP)	90	NA
Perkinsville (CDP)	33	NA
Perryville (CDP)	111	99648
Peters Creek	NA	99790
Petersburg (1910)	3,001	99833
Pilot Point (CDP)	66	99649
Pilot Station (1969)	323	99650
Pitkas Point (CDP)	88	99695
Platinum (1975)	55	99651
Point Baker (CDP)	90	99927

COMMUNITY	POPULATION	ZIP CODE	COMMUNITY	POPULATION	ZIP CODE	COMMUNITY	POPULATION	ZIP CODE
Point Hope (1966)	531	99766	Shishmaref (1969)	425	99772	Tuntutuliak (CDP)	216	99680
Point Lay (CDP)	68	99790	Shungnak (1967)	208	99773	Tununak (1975)	301	99681
Port Alexander (1974)	90	NA	Sitka (city and			Twin Hills (CDP)	70	99695
Port Clarence (CDP)	29	99790	borough)	7,927	99835	Two Rivers (CDP)	359	NA
Port Graham (CDP)	161	99603	Skagway (1900)	819	99840	Tyonek (CDP)	239	99682
Port Heiden (1972)	91	99549	Skwentna	NA	99667	Unalakleet (1974)	672	99684
Port Lions (1966)	218	99550	Slana (CDP)	49	99695	Unalaska (1942)	1,944	99685
Port Moller	NA	99695	Sleetmute (CDP)	107	99668	Upper Kalskag (1975)	128	NA
Port Walter	NA	99850	Soldotna (1967)	2,445	99669	Usibelli (CDP)	53	99787
Port Williams	NA	99697	South Naknek (CDP)	145	99670	Valdez (1901)	3,279	99686
Portage Creek (CDP)	48	NA	Sparrevohn Station (CDP)	26	NA	Venetie (CDP)	132	99781
Portlock (CDP)	31	99695	Stebbins (1969)	357	99671	Wainwright (1962)	410	99782
Prudhoe Bay (CDP)	50	99701	Sterling (CDP)	919	99672	Wales (1964)	143	99783
Quinhagak (1975)	409	99655	Stevens Village (CDP)	96	99774	Wasilla (1974)	1,928	99687
Rampart (CDP)	50	99767	Stony River (CDP)	62	99557	White Mountain (1969)	135	99784
Red Devil (CDP)	39	99656	Summit	NA	99775	Whittier (1969)	211	99501
Ruby (1973)	190	99768	Suntrana (CDP)	56	NA	Willow (CDP)	139	99688
Russian Mission (1970)	168	99657	Sutton (CDP)	182	NA	Wiseman	NA	99790
Saint George (CDP)	158	99660	Takotna (CDP)	48	99675	Wrangell (1903)	2,345	99929
Saint Marys (1967)	432	99658	Talkeetna (CDP)	264	99676	Yakutat (1948)	430	99689
Saint Michael (1969)	258	99659	Tanacross (CDP)	117	99776			
Saint Paul (1971)	591	99660	Tanana (1961)	463	99777			
Salamatof (CDP)	334	NA	Tatalina Station (CDP)	46	99695			
Salcha (CDP)	319	99714	Tatitlek (CDP)	68	99677			
Sand Point (1978)	697	99661	Tazlina (CDP)	31	NA			
Savoonga (1969)	530	99769	Telida (CDP)	33	NA			
Saxman (1930)	276	NA	Teller (1963)	229	99778			
Scammon Bay (1967)	249	99662	Tenakee Springs (1971)	132	99841			
Selawik (1977)	372	99770	Tetlin (CDP)	107	99779			
Seldovia (1945)	505	99663	Thorne Bay (CDP)	320	99950			
Seward (1912)	1,943	99664	Togiak (1969)	511	99678			
Shageluk (1970)	127	99665	Tok (CDP)	589	99780			
Shaktoolik (1969)	177	99771	Toksook Bay (1972)	331	99637			
Sheldon Point (1974)	103	99666	Tonsina (CDP)	135	NA			
Shemya Station (CDP)	600	99697	Tuluksak (1970)	234	99679			

INDUSTRIES

OIL AND GAS

Alaska's first exploratory oil well was drilled in 1898 on the Iniskin Peninsula, Cook Inlet, by Alaska Petroleum Company. According to the Alaska Oil and Gas Association, oil was encountered in this first hole at about 700 feet, but a water zone beneath the oil strata cut off the oil flow. Total depth of the well was approximately 1,000 feet.

The first commercial oil discovery was made in 1902 near Katalla, near the mouth of the Bering River east of Cordova. This field produced until 1933.

As early as 1921, oil companies surveyed land north of the Brooks Range for possible drilling sites. In 1923 the federal government created Naval Petroleum Reserve #4 (now known as National Petroleum Reserve-Alaska), a 23-million-acre area of Alaska's North Slope. Wartime needs speeded up exploration. In 1944 the navy began drilling operations on the North Slope and continued until 1953, but made no significant oil discoveries.

Atlantic Richfield discovered oil in 1957 on the Kenai Peninsula, at a depth of approximately two miles, about 20 miles northeast of Kenai. Later, Union Oil Company found a large gas field at Kalifonsky Beach, and Amoco found the first gas offshore at a location known as Middle Ground Shoals in Cook Inlet in 1962.

Currently, there are 14 production platforms in Cook Inlet, one of which produces only gas. Built to contend with extreme tides, siltation, and ice floes, the Cook Inlet platforms are in one of three successful areas of offshore oil production in the United States. Hundreds of miles of pipeline link the offshore platforms with onshore facilities at Kenai and Drift River. Gas reserves in the Kenai gas field are estimated to be the third largest in the United States. The deepest producing oil well in the state is at Soldotna Creek on the Kenai Peninsula; total depth is 17,689 feet. A fertilizer plant, largest of its kind on the West Coast, is located at Kenai. It uses natural gas to manufacture ammonia and urea. Two refineries are located at Kenai; a third is at North Pole near Fairbanks. Gasoline, diesel fuel, heavy fuel oil, JP-4, Jet A-50, and asphalt are produced for use within and outside of Alaska.

The Prudhoe Bay oil field, largest in North America, was discovered in 1968 by Atlantic-Richfield Company. Recoverable reserves are estimated to be 9.6 billion barrels of oil and 26 trillion cubic feet of natural gas. The field contains about one-quarter of the known petroleum reserves in the United States and each day produces 15 percent of the U.S. oil supply. The average daily production of 1.5 million barrels is transported via the trans-Alaska pipeline from Prudhoe Bay to Valdez. A $2 billion waterflood project is under way to maximize oil recovery by keeping the reservoir pressure constant as oil is produced. Sohio Alaska Petroleum Company operates the west half of the field and ARCO the east half. They operate for 12 participant companies.

The Kuparuk River Field, 40 miles west of Prudhoe Bay, is being developed by ARCO. The field went into production in mid-December 1981, and approximately 90,000 barrels a day is being delivered to the trans-Alaska pipeline. Production from Kuparuk is expected to reach 200,000 to 250,000 barrels a day in 1985.

The Alaska Natural Gas Transportation System — the Alaska gas pipeline — was authorized by the federal government in 1977. Estimated cost was $10 billion with a completion date in 1983. A two-year delay in the northern part of the project was announced in May 1982 by Northwest Alaskan, the consortium building the project. Cost estimates for the gas pipeline have risen to $40 billion with a completion date in 1990.

The natural gas pipeline route follows the trans-Alaska oil pipeline corridor to near Fairbanks, then the Alaska Highway through Alaska and Yukon Territory to British Columbia; branch lines extend into Alberta. Natural gas from Alberta gas reserves began flowing to West Coast states in October 1981. The total length of the gas pipeline (including proposed sections) is 4,800 miles.

Oil and gas leasing on state land in Alaska is managed by the Department of Natural Resources, Division of Minerals and Energy Management. The Secretary of the Interior is responsible for establishing oil and gas leasing on federal lands in Alaska, including the outer-continental shelf.

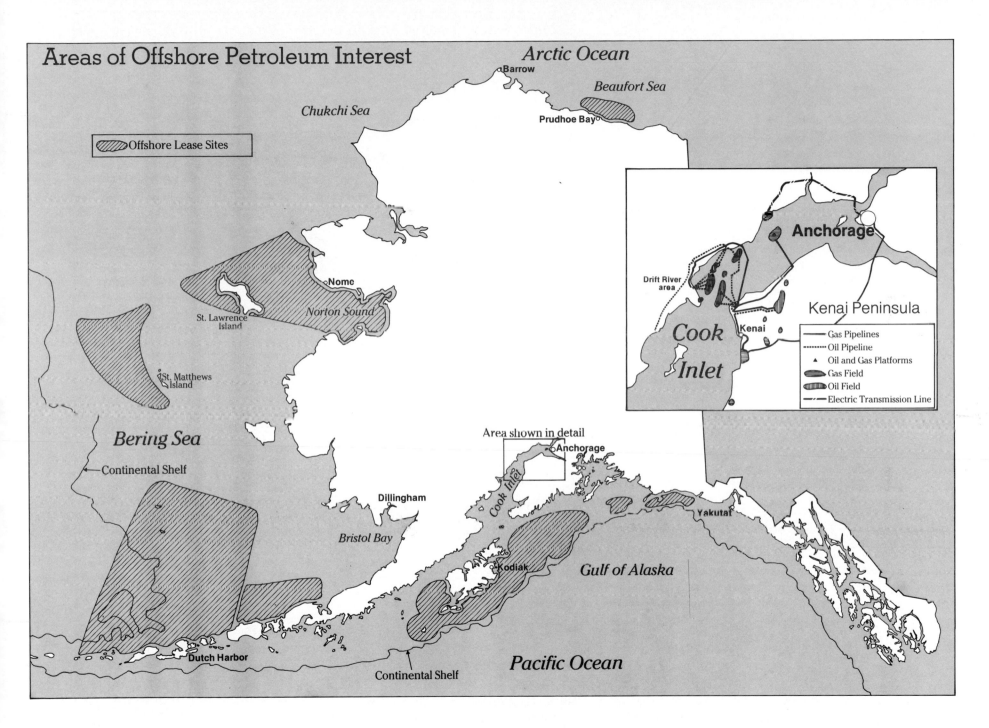

Areas of Offshore Petroleum Interest

Arctic Ocean

Beaufort Sea

Barrow

Chukchi Sea

Prudhoe Bay

⬚ Offshore Lease Sites

Nome

Norton Sound

St. Lawrence Island

St. Matthews Island

Bering Sea

Continental Shelf

Dillingham

Bristol Bay

Area shown in detail

Cook Inlet

Anchorage

Kodiak

Gulf of Alaska

Yakutat

Continental Shelf

Dutch Harbor

Pacific Ocean

Inset map

Anchorage

Drift River area

Cook Inlet

Kenai

Kenai Peninsula

— Gas Pipelines
···· Oil Pipeline
▲ Oil and Gas Platforms
⬭ Gas Field
⬮ Oil Field
—·— Electric Transmission Line

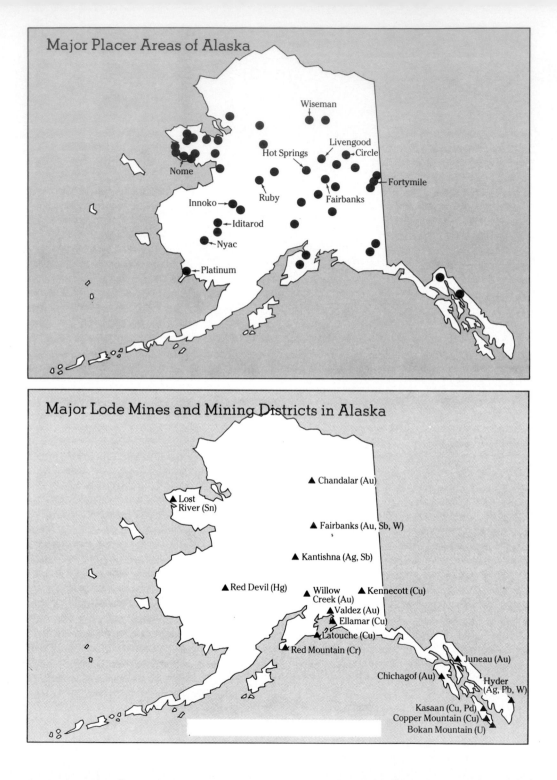

Major Placer Areas of Alaska

Wiseman

Livengood
Hot Springs
Circle

Nome

Fortymile

Innoko
Ruby
Fairbanks

Iditarod

Nyac

Platinum

Major Lode Mines and Mining Districts in Alaska

▲ Chandalar (Au)

▲ Lost
River (Sn)

▲ Fairbanks (Au, Sb, W)

▲ Kantishna (Ag, Sb)

▲ Red Devil (Hg)   ▲ Willow   ▲ Kennecott (Cu)
                       Creek (Au)
                     ▲ Valdez (Au)
                     ▲ Ellamar (Cu)
                   ▲ Latouche (Cu)
                 ▲ Red Mountain (Cr)

                                        ▲ Juneau (Au)

                        Chichagof (Au) ▲
                                        Hyder
                                        (Ag, Pb, W)

                            Kasaan (Cu, Pd) ▲
                          Copper Mountain (Cu) ▲
                            Bokan Mountain (U)

HARD-ROCK MINING

Mineral production in Alaska from 1880 to the present has included the following: antimony, asbestos, barite, chromite, coal, copper, crude petroleum, gold, graphite, gypsum, lead, marble/limestone, mercury, molybdenum, natural gas, nickel, platinum metals, sand and gravel, silver, stone, tin, tungsten, uranium, and zinc.

According to the Alaska Department of Natural Resources, Division of Geological and Geophysical Surveys, Alaska mineral production value in 1981 ranked as follows: natural gas, $83.3 million; gold, $54 million; sand and gravel, $128 million; other minerals, $21.5 million. Crude petroleum headed the list at $12,395,680,000.

FURS AND TRAPPING

Much of the state's trapping is done in the Yukon-Kuskokwim valleys and in the Arctic. It is seasonal work, so most trappers work summers at fishing or other employment.

Fur animals taken by trapping in Alaska are: beaver, coyote; red, arctic, white, or blue fox (red fox includes cross, black, or silver color phases); river (land) otter, lynx, marmot, marten, mink, muskrat, raccoon, squirrel (parka or ground, flying, and red), weasel, wolf, and wolverine. Trapping methods and possession and transportation of raw skins are subject to Alaska Department of Fish and Game regulations.

Prices for raw skins of Alaskan wild fur depend on the buyer, quality of fur, and market demand. Prices in 1981-82 ranged as follows: muskrat, 50¢ to $6; beaver, $25 to $65; arctic fox, $7 to $32; cross fox, $35 to $150; red fox, $55 to $130; wolf, $170 to $500; wolverine, $55 to $225; lynx, $125 to $500; marten, $15 to $75; mink, $10 to $85; river otter, $25 to $90.

TIMBER

According to the U.S. Department of Agriculture, Forest Service, 119 million acres of Alaska's 366 million acres of land surface are forested.

Alaska has two distinct forest ecosystems: the coastal rain forest and the interior forest. The vast interior forest covers 106 million acres, extending from the south slope of the Brooks Range to the Kenai Peninsula, and from Canada to Norton Sound. Over 22 million acres of white spruce, paper birch, quaking aspen, and balsam poplar stands are considered commercial forest land, comparing favorably in size and growth productivity with the forests of the lake states (Minnesota, Michigan and Wisconsin). The Interior's remoteness from markets and present land management policies have limited timber use to approximately 50 small local sawmills with limited export of cants and chips.

The coastal rain forests extend from Cook Inlet to the Alaska-Canada border south of Ketchikan and provide the bulk of commercial timber in Alaska today. Of the 13,247,000 acres of forested land, 5,749,000 acres contain commercial stands. Western hemlock, 70 percent of the total, and Sitka spruce, 25 percent of the total, provide the bulk of the timber harvest for domestic and export lumber and pulp markets. Western red cedar and Alaska (yellow) cedar make up the balance, with pine and other species also present.

According to the U.S. Department of Agriculture, Forest Service, Alaska timber harvest on public lands (state of Alaska, Bureau of Indian Affairs, Bureau of Land Management, and National Forest lands) in 1981 totaled 445,823,000 board feet.

FISHING, COMMERCIAL

Alaska's commercial fish production is greater than that of any other state in the country in value and second in terms of volume, according to the National Marine Fisheries Service.

Value and Volume of Alaska Fish and Shellfish Landings

YEAR	VALUE	VOLUME (in pounds)
1976	$219,071,000	600,203,000
1977	333,844,000	658,754,000
1978	482,207,000	767,167,000
1979	622,284,000	854,247,000
1980	561,751,000	983,664,000
1981	639,797,000	975,245,000

Source: *Fisheries of the United States 1981,* Department of Commerce

Value of Alaska's commercial fish landings in 1981 of $639.8 million was followed by: California, second in value at $275.2 million; Massachusetts, $196.9 million; Louisiana, $193.5 million; and Texas, $174.8 million.

Volume of Alaska's commercial fish landings in 1981 of 975.2 million pounds was second only to Louisiana, which recorded a volume of 1,168.6 million pounds in 1981. (In 1980, the United States was fourth in the world commercial fishery landings; Japan was first with 14 percent of the total 72.2 million metric tons, the USSR was second with 13 percent, and China was third with 6 percent.)

Kodiak was the leading U.S. port in terms of value in 1981, claiming $132.9 million in commercial fish landings. Los Angeles, California, was second with $110.5 million, and San Diego, California, was third with $83 million. Five other Alaska ports were ranked with the top 20 ports in the United States: Dutch Harbor was fifth with $57.6 million; Akutan

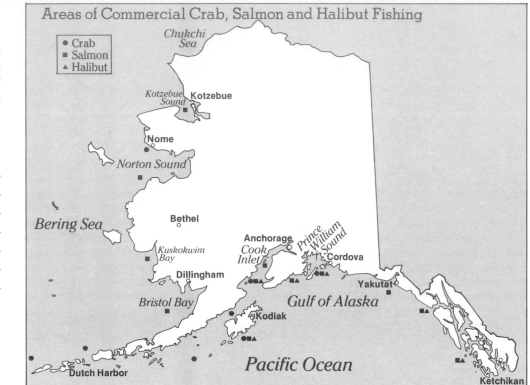

Areas of Commercial Crab, Salmon and Halibut Fishing

was thirteenth with $29.2 million; Ketchikan was fourteenth with $28.7 million; and Petersburg was nineteenth with $22 million.

Alaska pollock and other Alaska trawl fish landings by U.S. fishermen were 28 million pounds valued at $7.4 million. Additionally, U.S. fishermen participating in five joint ventures delivered 210 million pounds of trawl fish valued at $14.4 million to foreign processors.

Foreign fishing in Alaska waters, as in other U.S. waters, is governed by the Magnuson Fishery Conservation and Management Act of 1976. This act provides for the conservation and exclusive management by the U.S. of all fishery resources within the U.S. fishery conservation zone (except for highly migratory species of tuna). The U.S. fishery conservation zone established by the act extends from 3 nautical miles from shore to 200 nautical miles from shore. In addition, the act provides for exclusive management authority over continental shelf fishery resources and anadromous species (those that mature in the ocean then ascend streams to spawn in fresh water) beyond the 200-mile limit, except when they are within any recognized foreign nation's territorial sea. Foreign countries fishing within the U.S. zone do so under agreement with the U.S. and are subject to various fees. The 200-mile limit went into effect in 1977.

Foreign catch within the United States fishery conservation zone was 3.6 billion pounds in 1981, with Alaska supplying the

GOVERNMENT

largest share (91 percent) of the foreign catch, according to the National Marine Fisheries Service. The total foreign catch of trawl fish in Alaska waters was 3.3 billion pounds, about the same as in 1980. About 84 percent of the foreign catch (2.8 billion pounds) came from the Bering Sea and Aleutian Islands area; the remaining 512.7 million pounds came from the Gulf of Alaska.

King crab landings in Alaska in 1981 totaled 88.1 million pounds valued at $157.7 million. The Bering Sea landings accounted for 48.7 million pounds; Kodiak, 23.3 million pounds; and Dutch Harbor, almost 7 million pounds.

In the Bering Sea-Aleutian Islands area, 50.5 million pounds of *C. opilio* crab valued at $13.1 million were landed in 1981, and 30.4 million pounds of *C. bairdi* crab valued at $17.7 million.

Statewide totals for other shellfish landed in 1981 include the following: tanner crab, 107.5 million pounds; Dungeness, 14.9 million pounds; scallops, 889,777 pounds; and octopus, 53,084 pounds. Alaska landings of shrimp (trawl and pot) were 27.7 million pounds, valued at $7.5 million.

Halibut landings off Alaska totaled 26.4 million pounds in 1981, up from 1980's 19 million pounds. The Alaska catch of halibut accounted for 99 percent of U.S. landings. The average price for domestic halibut was 76¢ per pound.

According to the National Marine Fisheries Service, salmon was the second most important commercial species in quantity and value in 1981.

Alaska is represented in the U.S. Congress by two senators and one representative.

A governor and lieutenant governor are elected by popular vote for four-year terms on the same ticket. The governor is termed strong because of extensive powers given under the constitution. He administers 14 major departments: Administration, Commerce and Economic Development, Community and Regional Affairs, Education, Environmental Conservation, Fish and Game, Health and Social Services, Labor, Law, Military Affairs, Natural Resources, Public Safety, Revenue, and Transportation and Public Facilities.

The legislature is bicameral, with 20 senators elected for four-year terms, and 40 representatives for two-year terms. The judiciary consists of a state supreme court, superior court, district courts, and magistrates.

Local government is by a system of organized boroughs, much like counties in other states. Several areas of the state are not included in any borough because of sparse population. Boroughs generally provide a more limited number of services than cities. There are three classes. First- and second-class boroughs have two mandatory powers: education and land use planning. The major difference between the two classes is how they may acquire other powers. Both classes have separately elected borough assemblies and school boards. A third-class borough has one mandatory power: operation of public schools. All boroughs may assess, levy, and collect real and personal property taxes.

Incorporated cities are small units of local government, serving one community. There are two classes. First-class cities, generally urban areas, have six-member councils and a separately elected mayor. Taxing authority is somewhat broader than second-class cities,

and responsibilities are broader. A first-class city that has adopted a home rule charter is called a home rule city; adoption allows the city to revise its ordinances, such that the powers it assumes are those not prohibited by law or charter. Second-class cities, generally places with fewer than 400 people, are governed by a seven-member council, one of whom serves as mayor. Taxing authority is limited. A borough and all cities located within it may unite in a single unit of government called a unified municipality.

There is also one community organized under federal law. Originally an Indian reservation, Metlakatla was organized so municipal services could effectively be provided to its residents.

In 1981 there were 153 incorporated municipalities: 3 unified home rule municipalities, 1 home rule borough, 6 second-class boroughs, 1 third-class borough, 11 home rule cities, 21 first-class cities, 110 second-class cities and one community, Metlakatla, organized under federal law.

Borough Addresses and Contact

The City and Borough of Juneau
Contact: City-Borough Manager
155 South Seward Street
Juneau 99801
Telephone: 586-3300

Kodiak Island Borough
*Contact: Borough Mayor or
Borough Clerk*
P.O. Box 1246
Kodiak 99615
Telephone: 486-5736

Kenai Peninsula Borough
Contact: Borough Clerk
P.O. Box 850
Soldotna 99669
Telephone: 262-4441

Municipality of Anchorage
*Contact: Mayor's Office or
Manager's Office*
632 West Sixth Avenue
Pouch 6-650
Anchorage 99502
Telephone: 264-4431

Bristol Bay Borough
Contact: Borough Clerk
P.O. Box 189
Naknek 99633
Telephone: 268-4224

Haines Borough
Contact: Borough Secretary
Box H
Haines 99827
Telephone: 766-2711

City and Borough of Sitka
Contact: Administrator
P.O. Box 79
Sitka 99835
Telephone: 747-3294

Ketchikan Gateway Borough
Contact: Borough Manager
344 Front Street
Ketchikan 99901
Telephone: 225-6151

Matanuska-Susitna Borough
Contact: Borough Manager
Box B
Palmer 99645
Telephone: 745-4801

North Slope Borough
Contact: Borough Mayor
P.O. Box 69
Barrow 99723
Telephone: 852-2611

Fairbanks North Star Borough
Contact: Clerk
512 Second Avenue
P.O. Box 1267
Fairbanks 99701
Telephone: 452-4761

AGRICULTURE

Agricultural production in Alaska is still confined to a relatively small area of the state's total acreage. The availability of new agricultural land continues to be tight. However, state land sales since 1978 have placed more than 90,000 acres of potential agricultural land into private ownership. Most of this acreage is in the Delta Junction area with tracts of land ranging up to 3,200 for the purpose of grain farming.

In 1980 the total value of Alaska's agricultural products was $9,659,580 ($421,000 higher than in 1979); crops accounted for $5.8 million of the total, livestock and poultry for $3.9 million. Broken down by region, the Matanuska Valley accounted for 67 percent of the total value; the Tanana Valley, 23 percent; the Kenai Peninsula, 6 percent; southwestern Alaska, 3 percent; and Southeast, 1 percent.

According to the state Division of Agriculture, the value and volume of principal crops in 1980 were:

	VALUE (in sales)	VOLUME (in thousands)
Milk	$2,244,000	12.5 lbs.
Hay	2,100,000	15.0 tons
Potatoes	1,463,000	77.0 cwt
Barley	1,017,000	339.0 bu
Vegetables	642,500	23.3 cwt
Silage	484,000	12.4 tons
Eggs	412,425	367.0 doz.
Beef & Veal	324,000	767.0 lbs.
Pork	221,000	232.0 lbs.
Oats	81,000	26.1 bu

Sales of reindeer meat and by-products in 1977, the last year for which figures are available, were valued at $421,000. Most of the state's reindeer are located on the Seward Peninsula and Nunivak Island.

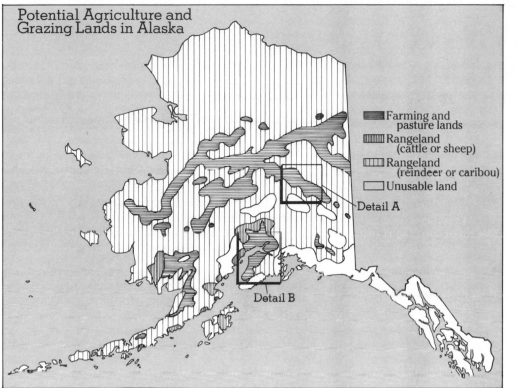

Potential Agriculture and Grazing Lands in Alaska

Legend:
- Farming and pasture lands
- Rangeland (cattle or sheep)
- Rangeland (reindeer or caribou)
- Unusable land

Detail A
Detail B

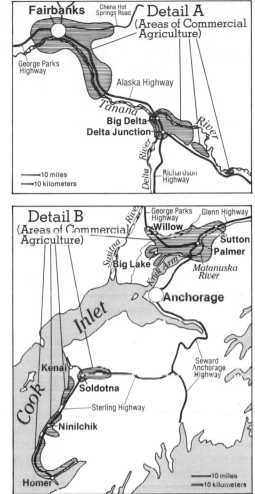

Detail A (Areas of Commercial Agriculture)

Fairbanks — Chena Hot Springs Road
George Parks Highway
Alaska Highway
Tanana River
Big Delta
Delta Junction
Delta River
Richardson Highway

10 miles
10 kilometers

Detail B (Areas of Commercial Agriculture)

George Parks Highway
Glenn Highway
Willow
Susitna River
Big Lake
Knik Arm
Sutton
Palmer
Matanuska River
Cook Inlet
Anchorage
Kenai
Soldotna
Sterling Highway
Seward Anchorage Highway
Ninilchik
Homer

10 miles
10 kilometers

Alaska has experienced growth in the number of small farms through state sales of smaller tracts and the use of farming as a supplement to other income. In 1978, 202 farms of from 1 to 49 acres accounted for almost 67 percent of the harvested cropland.

The Matanuska Valley sells primarily to Anchorage and military markets. Dairy farming is the dominant income source, including feed crops for cows. The valley has a 120-day growing season that includes up to 19 hours of sunlight daily (occasionally producing giant-sized vegetables), warm temperatures, and moderate rainfall. During most years, supplemental irrigation is required. Residential development in the Matanuska Valley has contributed to a decline in the amount of agricultural land.

In the Tanana Valley the growing season is shorter than in the Matanuska Valley, with 90 frost-free days, and low precipitation levels, making irrigation necessary for some crops. However, this region has the greatest agricultural potential, with warmer temperatures during the growing season and the presence of large tracts of reasonably flat land with brush rather than forest growth. The promotion of grain farming in the Tanana Valley has been a major effort by the state. The Delta Barley Project I in 1978 disposed of 65,000 acres of land in the Delta Junction area by lottery. The Delta II auction in 1982 disposed of an additional 24,000 acres of land.

The Kenai Peninsula produces some beef, hay and potatoes. Kodiak Island produces more beef than any other area in the state.

The islands of Umnak and Unalaska provided graze for 3,900 sheep for wool in 1980, the smallest number in many years. There were 27,000 head in 1970.

Based on Soil Conservation Service information, there are at least 15 million acres of potential farmland in Alaska suitable for raising crops, plus 108 million acres of range for livestock grazing, most of which is suitable only for reindeer. There were 960 persons engaged in farm labor in Alaska in 1980.

151

TRANSPORTATION

HIGHWAYS

As of December 31, 1981, the state Department of Transportation and Public Facilities showed 13,698.9 miles of highways, including those in national parks and forests (2,004), and 1,416 miles of ferry routes. Of the total, 3,092.3 miles were unpaved, 2,384.7 miles were paved, 834.4 were municipal roads, 1,349.1 were borough roads, and 2,618.3 were listed as "other."

Alaska Highway

The highway runs 1,520 miles through Canada and Alaska from Milepost 0 at Dawson Creek, British Columbia, to Fairbanks, Alaska. (The highway from Milepost 1422 at Delta Junction to Milepost 1520 at Fairbanks shares a common alignment with the Richardson Highway.)

By agreement between the governments of Canada and the United States, the highway was built in eight months by the U.S. Army Corps of Engineers and dedicated in November 1942. Crews worked south from Delta Junction, Alaska, north and south from Whitehorse, Yukon Territory, and north from Dawson Creek, British Columbia.

Two major sections of the highway were connected on September 23, 1942, at Contact Creek, Milepost 588.1, where the Thirty-fifth Engineer Combat Regiment working west from Fort Nelson met the 340th Engineer General Service Regiment working east from Whitehorse. The last link in the highway was completed November 20, when the Ninety-seventh Engineer General Service Regiment, heading east from Tanacross, met the Eighteenth Engineer Combat Regiment at Milepost 1200.9, coming ,northwest from Kluane Lake. On this day a pioneer form of highway was completed. A ceremony com-

memorating the event was held at Soldiers Summit, approximately 100 miles east of the Alaska-Yukon border, and the first truck to negotiate the entire highway left that day from Soldiers Summit and arrived in Fairbanks the next day.

The highway was built to relieve Alaska from the wartime hazards of shipping and to supply a land route for wartime equipment. It was then turned over to civilian contractors for widening and graveling, replacing log bridges with steel, and rerouting at many

points. Construction continues on the Alaska Highway today as more miles are paved or hard-surfaced, and stretches of road improved. The Alaska portion of the Alaska Highway is paved (299 miles) and approximately 400 miles in Canada are paved; the remainder is either hard-surfaced or gravel.

Driving the Alaska Highway requires a few preparations like protecting your car against gravel and carrying some spare parts. A partial list of spares includes: trailer bearings, fan belts, tires, jumper cables, siphoning hose, all-

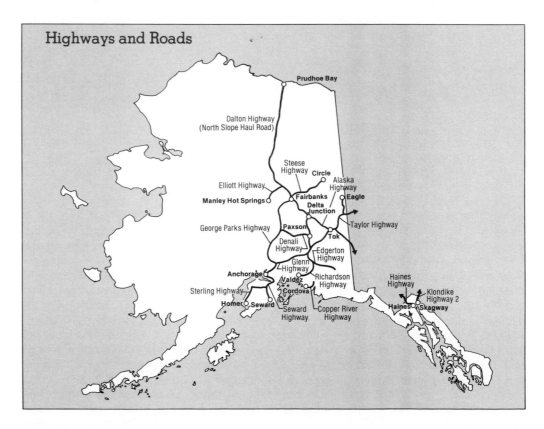

Highways and Roads

Alaska Mileage Chart

	Alaska Boundary	Anchorage	Chicago, IL	Circle	Dawson Creek, BC	Delta Junction	Eagle	Edmonton, AB	Fairbanks	Glennallen	Great Falls, MT	Haines	Haines Jct., YT	Homer	Livengood	Los Angeles, CA	New York, NY	Palmer	Paxson	Portage	Seattle, WA	Seward	Tok	Valdez	Whitehorse, YT
Alaska Boundary		421	3506	463	1221	201	242	1591	298	232	2106	364	205	648	380	3208	4347	373	274	469	2063	550	93	347	304
Anchorage	421		3927	523	1642	340	503	2012	358	189	2527	785	626	227	440	3629	4768	40	259	48	2484	129	328	304	725
Chicago, IL	3506	3927		3969	2285	3707	3748	1915	3804	3738	1400	3460	3301	4154	3886	2095	840	3879	3780	3975	2103	4056	3599	3853	3202
Circle	463	523	3969		1684	262	545	2054	165	413	2569	827	668	750	223	3671	4810	483	343	571	2526	652	370	528	767
Dawson Creek, BC	1221	1642	2285	1684		1422	1463	370	1519	1453	885	1175	1016	1869	1601	1987	3126	1594	1495	1690	842	1771	1314	1568	917
Delta Junction	201	340	3707	262	1422		283	1792	97	151	2307	565	406	567	179	3409	4548	292	81	388	2264	469	108	266	505
Eagle	242	503	3748	545	1463	283		1833	380	314	2348	606	447	730	462	3450	4589	455	356	551	2305	632	175	429	546
Edmonton, AB	1591	2012	1915	2054	370	1792	1833		1889	1823	515	1545	1386	2239	1971	2088	2756	1964	1865	2060	943	2141	1684	1938	1287
Fairbanks	298	358	3804	165	1519	97	380	1889		248	2404	662	503	585	82	3506	4645	389	178	406	2361	487	205	363	602
Glennallen	232	189	3738	413	1453	151	314	1823	248		2338	596	437	416	330	3440	4579	141	70	237	2295	318	139	115	536
Great Falls, MT	2106	2527	1400	2569	885	2307	2348	515	2404	2338		2060	1901	2754	2486	1848	2241	2479	2380	2575	703	2656	2199	2453	1802
Haines	364	785	3460	827	1175	565	606	1545	662	596	2060		159	1012	744	3162	4301	737	638	833	2017	914	457	711	258
Haines Jct., YT	205	626	3301	668	1016	406	447	1386	503	437	1901	159		853	585	3003	4142	578	479	674	1858	755	298	552	99
Homer	648	227	4154	750	1869	567	730	2239	585	416	2754	1012	853		667	3856	4995	267	486	179	2711	172	555	531	952
Livengood	380	440	3886	223	1601	179	462	1971	82	330	2486	744	585	667		3588	4727	400	260	488	2443	569	287	445	684
Los Angeles, CA	3208	3629	2095	3671	1987	3409	3450	2088	3506	3440	1848	3162	3003	3856	3588		2915	3581	3482	3677	1145	3758	3301	3555	2904
New York, NY	4347	4768	840	4810	3126	4548	4589	2756	4645	4579	2241	4301	4142	4995	4727	2915		4720	4621	4816	2944	4897	4440	4694	4043
Palmer	373	40	3879	483	1594	292	455	1964	389	141	2479	737	578	267	400	3581	4720		211	88	2436	169	280	256	677
Paxson	274	259	3780	343	1495	81	356	1865	178	70	2380	638	479	486	260	3482	4621	211		307	2337	388	181	185	578
Portage	469	48	3975	571	1690	388	551	2060	406	237	2575	833	674	179	488	3677	4816	88	307		2532	81	376	352	773
Seattle, WA	2063	2484	2103	2526	842	2264	2305	943	2361	2295	703	2017	1858	2711	2443	1145	2944	2436	2337	2532		2613	2156	2410	1759
Seward	550	129	4056	652	1771	469	632	2141	487	318	2656	914	755	172	569	3758	4897	169	388	81	2613		457	433	854
Tok	93	328	3599	370	1314	108	175	1684	205	139	2199	457	298	555	287	3301	4440	280	181	376	2156	457		254	397
Valdez	347	304	3853	528	1568	266	429	1938	363	115	2453	711	552	531	445	3555	4694	256	185	352	2410	433	254		651
Whitehorse, YT	304	725	3202	767	917	505	546	1287	602	536	1802	258	99	952	684	2904	4043	677	578	773	1759	854	397	651	

purpose plastic tape, wire, strong glue, selection of sheet-metal screws, rubber washers of various sizes, tire chains, tire pump, tire repair kit, tire breakdown tools, complete tool kit, points, condenser, and spark plugs.

Preparation for gravel: Protect headlights with clear plastic covers made specifically for that purpose. In addition, you might consider a wire-mesh screen across the front of your vehicle to protect paint and radiator from flying rocks.

Substituting metal for rubber in the fuel lines underneath the car will provide longer wear. The rubber boots on axle joints of front-wheel-drive vehicles should be checked frequently. Rotating the tires every 1,000 miles or so will extend tire life.

There is practically no way to protect the windshield, although motorists have experimented with screen shields that do not seriously impair their vision. Larger towns throughout the Northland have auto glass repair shops.

Gas tanks are often damaged. To protect them insert a rubber mat between gas tank and securing straps — old rubber floor mats and truck flaps work well.

If your car should break down on the highway and tow truck service is needed, normally you will be able to flag down a passing motorist. Travelers in the North are especially helpful in such situations and the etiquette of the country requires one to stop. If you are the only person traveling in the disabled car, be sure to leave a note on your windshield indicating when you left the car and in what direction you planned to travel. This is particularly important when traveling in winter.

Dust protection: Along the Alaska Highway dust is at its worst during dry spells, following heavy rain (which disturbs the road surface), and in construction areas. If you encounter much dust, check your air filter frequently. To help keep dust out of your vehicle, try to keep air pressure in the car by closing all windows and turning on the fan. Filtered heating and air-conditioning ducts in a vehicle bring in much less dust than open windows or vents. Mosquito netting placed over the heater/fresh air intake and flow-through ventilation will also help eliminate dust.

AIR TRAVEL

Alaska is the "flyingest" state in the Union; the only practical way to reach many areas of rural Alaska is by airplane. According to the Federal Aviation Administration, Alaska Region, by December 1981 there were approximately 10,000 registered pilots — one out of every 40 Alaskans — and 7,450 registered aircraft — one for every 54 Alaskans. This figure is approximately six times as many pilots per capita and 12 times as many airplanes per capita as compared to the rest of the United States.

Lake Hood in Anchorage is one of the largest and busiest seaplane bases in the world. In 1981, 73,445 takeoffs and landings were recorded.

Merrill Field in Anchorage had 310,217 takeoffs and landings recorded in 1981 making it the 36th busiest airport in the United States for the year.

Alaska, with 516 airports and airstrips, 122 officially recognized seaplane landing sites, and 33 heliports, ranks fourth in the nation in the number of landing sites. Only Texas (1,375), Illinois (942), and California (825), have more. In addition, there are numerous remote landing strips.

For pilots who wish to fly their own planes to Alaska, a booklet titled *Flight Tips for Alaskan Tourists* may be obtained from the Federal Aviation Administration, Flight Standards District Office #63, 6601 South Airpark Place, Suite 216, Anchorage 99502.

According to the Alaska Transportation Commission, certified air carriers with operating rights within Alaska as of February 1982 included: 227 air taxi operators; 12 contract air carriers; 3 postal contract carriers; 14 subcontract carriers; and 35 scheduled air carriers.

Air taxi operators are found in most Alaskan communities and aircraft can be chartered for transportation or for flightseeing. A wide range of aircraft is used for charter and scheduled passenger service in Alaska. The large interstate airlines — Alaska, Northwest, Western, and Wien — use jets (DC-10s, 727s, 737s, 747s); Reeve Aleutian flies Electras, YS-11s, DC-4s and DC-6s. Prop jets and single or twin engine prop planes on wheels, skis, and floats are used for most intrastate travel. Here are just a few of the types of aircraft flown in Alaska: DC-3s, 19-passenger Twin Otter, 10-passenger Britten-Norman Islander, 7-passenger Grumman Goose (amphibious), 5-passenger Cessna 185, 9-passenger twin engine Piper Navajo Chieftain, 5- to 8-passenger Beaver, 3- to 4-passenger Cessna 180, 5- to 6-passenger Cessna 206, and single-passenger Super Cub.

U.S. carriers providing interstate passenger service are: Alaska Airlines, Northwest Orient Airlines, Western Airlines, Wien Air Alaska, and Reeve Aleutian. These carriers and Flying Tigers also provide freight service between Anchorage and Seattle. Reeve Aleutian Airways provides freight and passenger service between Cold Bay and Seattle.

Foreign carriers servicing Alaska through the Anchorage gateway are: Air France, British Airways, KLM Royal Dutch Airlines,

Korean Airlines, Lufthansa German Airlines, Northwest Orient Airlines (Japan), Sabena-Belgian World Airlines, and Scandinavian Airlines.

RAILROADS

There are two railroads in Alaska: The Alaska Railroad and the White Pass & Yukon Route.

The Alaska Railroad is the northernmost railroad in North America and the only one owned by the United States government, although efforts are under way to transfer ownership to the state of Alaska. The ARR rolls on 470 miles of mainline track from the ports of Seward and Whittier, to Anchorage on Cook Inlet, and Fairbanks in the Interior.

The Alaska Railroad began in 1912 with the appointment by Congress of a commission to study transportation problems in Alaska. In March 1914 the president authorized railroad lines in the Territory of Alaska to connect open harbors on the southern coast of Alaska with the Interior. The Alaska Engineering Commission surveyed possible railroad routes in 1914 and, in April 1915, President Woodrow Wilson announced the selection of a route from Seward north 412 miles to the Tanana River (where Nenana is now located), with branch lines to Matanuska coal fields. The main line was later extended to Fairbanks. Construction of the railroad began in 1915. On July 15, 1923, President Warren G. Harding drove the golden spike — signifying completion of the railroad — at Nenana.

Run by the Department of Transportation, the railroad offers year-round passenger, freight, and vehicle service. The ARR features flag-stop service along the Anchorage-to-Fairbanks corridor, as well as summer express trains to Denali National Park and Preserve. For information contact the Alaska Railroad, Pouch 7-2111, Anchorage 99510.

The privately owned White Pass & Yukon Route is a narrow-gauge link between Skagway, Alaska, and Whitehorse, Yukon Territory. At the time it was built — 1898 to 1900 — it was the farthest north any railroad had operated in North America. It has one of the steepest railroad grades in North America, climbing to 2,885 feet at White Pass in only 20 miles of track.

FERRIES

The state Department of Transportation, Division of Marine Highway Systems, provides year-round scheduled ferry service for passengers and vehicles to communities in southeastern and southwestern Alaska. (The southeastern and southwestern Alaska state ferry systems do not connect with each other.)

A fleet of seven ferries on the southeastern system connects the ports of Ketchikan, Metlakatla, Hollis, Wrangell, Petersburg, Kake, Sitka, Angoon, Pelican, Hoonah, Tenakee Springs, Juneau, Haines, and Skagway. These southeastern communities — with the exception of Haines and Skagway — are accessible only by ferry or by airplane. The ferry system also provides regularly scheduled service from Prince Rupert, British Columbia, and Seattle, Washington, to southeastern Alaska. The vessels of the southeastern system are the *Aurora, Columbia, Chilkat, LeConte, Malaspina, Matanuska* and *Taku.*

Southwestern Alaska is served by two ferries. The *Tustumena* serves Seward, Port Lions, Kodiak, Homer, Seldovia, Cordova, and Valdez, with limited summer service to Chignik, Sand Point, King Cove, Cold Bay, and Dutch Harbor. In summer, the *Bartlett* provides service between Valdez, Cordova, and Whittier.

Scheduled state ferry service to southeastern Alaska began in 1963; ferry service to Kodiak Island began in 1964. The first three ferries of the Alaska ferry fleet were the *Malaspina, Matanuska,* and *Taku;* the names were selected by then governor William A. Egan.

Reservations are required for vehicles and staterooms on all sailings. Passenger reservations are required on some sailings. The address of the main office of the Alaska Marine Highway Systems is Pouch R, Juneau 99811; phone (907) 465-3941 or 465-3940.

ALASKA STATE FERRY DATA

VESSEL	BEGAN SERVICE	LENGTH (feet)	SPEED (knots)	PASSENGERS	VEHICLES	CABINS
Aurora	1977	235	14	250	47	0
Bartlett	1969	193	14	170	38	0
Chilkat	1959	99	10	75	15	0
Columbia	1973	418	19	1,000	180	96
LeConte	1974	235	14	250	47	0
Malaspina	1963*	408	16.5	750	120	86
Matanuska	1963	408	16.5	750	120	112
Taku	1963	352	16	500	105	30
Tustumena	1964	296	14	220	50	27

*Lengthened and renovated 1972.

FLORA

TREES AND SHRUBS

According to the U.S. Department of Agriculture, the number of native tree species in Alaska is less than in any other state. Species of trees and shrubs in Alaska fall under the following families: yew, pine, cypress, willow, bayberry, birch, mistletoe, gooseberry, rose, maple, elaeagnus, ginseng, dogwood, crowberry, pyrola, heath, dispensia, honeysuckle, and composite.

Commercial timber species include white spruce, Sitka spruce, western hemlock, mountain hemlock, western red cedar, Alaska cedar, balsam poplar, black cottonwood, quaking aspen, and paper birch.

Rare tree species include the Pacific yew, Pacific silver fir, subalpine fir, silver willow and Hooker willow.

WILD FLOWERS

Alaska's wild flowers are sometimes flamboyant; most commonly they are small and delicate. Approximately 1,500 plant species occur in the state, including trees, shrubs, ferns, grasses and sedges.

Alpine regions are particularly rich in flora and some of the species are quite rare. Eagle Summit (Steese Highway), Thompson Pass (Richardson Highway), Maclaren Summit (Denali Highway), Polychrome Pass (Denali National Park), Turnagain Pass (Seward Highway), Eklutna Flats (north of Anchorage), and Hatcher Pass (near Wasilla) are wonderful botanizing areas and are all easily accessible

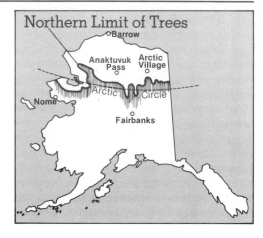
Northern Limit of Trees
Barrow
Anaktuvuk Pass
Arctic Village
Arctic Circle
Nome
Fairbanks

by car. There are, of course, many other regions to delight the wild flower fancier.

Alaska's official state flower, the forget-me-not *(Myosotis alpestris)*, is a delicate little beauty found throughout much of the state in alpine meadows and along streams. Growing to 18 inches tall, forget-me-nots are recognized by their bright, bright blue petals surrounding a yellow "eye." A northern "cousin," the arctic forget-me-not *(Eritrichium aretioides)*, grows in sandy soil on the tundra or in the mountains, and reaches only four inches in height.

BERRIES

Edible wild berries are abundant in Alaska, with the lowbush cranberry, or lingonberry (*Vaccinium vitis-idaea*), being perhaps the most widespread of the approximately 50 species of wild berries found in the state. Wild strawberries, blueberries, raspberries, cloudberries, nagoonberries, salmonberries, crowberries, watermelon berries, currants and rose hips all ripen in summer and early fall. Highbush cranberries can be found on the bush even in the dead of winter. They provide a refreshing treat to the hiker smart enough to pick the frozen berries.

Rose hips are an outstanding source of vitamin C, a few berries offering as much as an orange. The vitamin C content increases the farther north the berries are found.

POISONOUS PLANTS

There are poisonous plants in Alaska but not many considering the total quantity of plant species growing in the state. Baneberry *(Actaea rubra)*, water hemlock *(Cicuta douglasii* and *C. mackenzieana)*, and fly agaric mushroom *(Amanita muscaria)* are the most dangerous. Be sure you have properly identified plants before harvesting for food. Alaska has no plants poisonous to the touch such as poison ivy and poison oak, found in almost all other states.

FAUNA

MAMMALS

Large Land Mammals

Black bear — Highest densities found in southeastern, Prince William Sound, and southcentral coastal mountains and lowlands. Also occur in interior and western Alaska. Absent from southeastern islands north of Frederick Sound (primarily Admiralty, Baranof, and Chichagof) and Kodiak archipelago. Not commonly found west of about Naknek Lake on the Alaska Peninsula, in the Aleutian Islands, or on the open tundra sloping into the Bering Sea and Arctic Ocean.

Brown/grizzly bear — Found in most of Alaska. Absent from southeastern islands south of Frederick Sound and from most of the Aleutians.

Polar bear — There are two groups in Alaska's Arctic rim: an eastern group found largely in the Beaufort Sea, and a western group found in the Chukchi Sea between Alaska and Siberia. The latter group are the largest polar bears in the world (some old males exceed 1,500 pounds).

American bison — In 1928, 23 bison were transplanted from Montana to Delta Junction to restore Alaska's bison population which had been wiped out some 500 years before. Today, several hundred bison graze near Delta Junction; other herds are at Farewell, Chitina, and Nabesna.

Barren Ground caribou — About 13 distinct herds: Adak, Alaska Peninsula, Arctic, Beaver, Chisana, Delta, Kenai, McKinley, Mentasta, Mulchatna, Nelchina, Porcupine, and Fortymile. Porcupine and Fortymile herds range into Canada.

Sitka blacktail deer — Coastal rain forests of Southeast; expanded by transplants to Yakutat area, Prince William Sound, and Kodiak and Afognak islands.

Roosevelt elk — Transplanted in 1928 from Olympic Peninsula, Washington, to Raspberry and Afognak islands.

Moose — Found from the Unuk River in Southeast to the arctic slope. Most abundant in second-growth birch forests, on timber line plateaus, and along major rivers of Southcentral and Interior. Not found on islands in Prince William Sound or Bering Sea, most major islands in Southeast nor on Kodiak or Aleutians group.

Mountain goat — Found in mountains throughout Southeast and north and west along coastal mountains to Cook Inlet and Kenai Peninsula; successfully transplanted to Kodiak and Baranof islands.

Musk ox — First transplanted to Nunivak Island and from there to arctic slope around Kavik, Seward Peninsula, Cape Thompson, and Nelson Island.

Dall sheep — Found in all major mountain ranges in Alaska except the Aleutian Range south of Iliamna Lake.

Wolf — Found throughout Alaska except Bering Sea islands, some southeastern and Prince William Sound islands, and most of the Aleutian Islands. Classified as big game and as fur bearer. Inhabits a variety of climates and terrains.

Wolverine — Found throughout Alaska and on some southeastern islands; abundant in the Interior and on the Alaska Peninsula. Shy, solitary creatures; not abundant in comparison with other fur bearers. Member of the weasel family. Classified as big game and as fur bearer.

Fur Bearers

Beaver — Found in most of mainland Alaska from Brooks Range to middle of Alaska Peninsula. Abundant in some major mainland river drainages in Southeast and on Yakutat forelands. Successfully transplanted to Kodiak area. Beaver dams are sometimes destroyed to allow salmon upstream; however, the beavers can rebuild their dams quickly and usually do so on the same site.

Coyote — First recorded in southeastern mainland. Believed to have established themselves in interior Alaska around 1930. Common in Tanana, Copper, Matanuska, and Susitna river drainages and on the Kenai Peninsula.

Arctic fox — The fur bearer of the arctic slope, found almost entirely along arctic coast and south along west coast to near Bristol Bay.

157

Introduced to Pribilof and Aleutian islands; occurs naturally on Saint Lawrence and Nunivak islands. Color phases are white and blue.

Red fox — Found throughout Alaska except for most of Southeast and Prince William Sound. Most are found in major mainland drainages of Interior; introduced to Aleutian Islands. Common color is golden; other color phases are pure black, black with silver-tipped hairs, and cross (brownish-yellow with dark band across shoulders and down back).

Lynx — Great Dane-sized relative of the bobcat; preys mainly on snowshoe hare. Found throughout the state except on the extreme arctic slope, the Aleutian Islands, and southeastern islands, the Yukon-Kuskokwim Delta and southern Alaska Peninsula.

Hoary marmot — Found throughout most of Alaska in mountainous regions near or above timber line. Not found in lower elevations such as Seward Peninsula, Yukon-Kuskokwim Delta, and lower Alaska Peninsula. Makes a distinctive sharp whistle sound when alarmed.

Marten — Found throughout timbered Alaska in mature stands of spruce. Introduced to Prince of Wales, Baranof, Chichagof, and Afognak islands. Absent from islands of Prince William Sound, from Kodiak Island, and north of Brooks Range, treeless sections of Alaska Peninsula, Yukon-Kuskokwim Delta and Aleutian Islands.

Mink — Common throughout Alaska except for arctic slope, Kodiak archipelago, Aleutian Islands and Bering Sea islands. Greatest concentration on island and mainland beaches of Southeast. Favors brushy streams and ponds or saltwater beaches.

Muskrat — Found throughout mainland Alaska south of Brooks Range except for Alaska Peninsula west of Ugashik Lakes. Concentrations occur on Yukon and Minto flats, Tetlin Lakes, Yukon-Kuskokwim Delta and Kotzebue Sound area. Introduced to Kodiak, Afognak, and Raspberry islands. Found near Juneau, Haines, and Stikine River in Southeast. Live near water, usually around marshes, lakes, ponds, and rivers, in houses built of rushes and other water plants.

River (land) otter — Found in streams and lakes throughout state and inland bays and tidal estuaries. Not found on Aleutian or Bering Sea islands or on arctic coastal plain east of Point Lay. Member of the weasel family.

Sea otter — Almost wiped out by hunting in the 1800s, sea otters were given protection in 1911. Today, an estimated 125,000 sea otters are found in Alaska in Prince William Sound, Cook Inlet, Kodiak area, along the Alaska Peninsula and throughout the Aleutians. Also found in Southeast.

Arctic ground squirrel — Found throughout much of Alaska in well-drained tundra; most abundant in mountainous terrain. Absent from Southeast, Yukon-Kuskokwim Delta, Prince William Sound, Kodiak archipelago, and central Brooks Range.

Northern flying squirrel — Inhabits fairly dense usually coniferous forests from southeastern north to southcentral and interior Alaska. Nocturnal mammals, they glide rather than fly by extending skin folds between front and rear legs.

Red squirrel — Found in spruce forests, especially along rivers, from Southeast north to the Brooks Range. Absent from Seward Peninsula, Yukon-Kuskokwim Delta, and Alaska Peninsula south of Naknek River.

Weasel — Least weasel and short-tailed weasel are found throughout Alaska, except for Bering Sea and Aleutian islands. Short-tailed weasels are brown with white underparts in summer, becoming snow-white in winter (designated ermine).

Other Small Mammals

Bat — There are five common bat species in Alaska.

Northern hare (or tundra hare) — Inhabits western and northern coastal Alaska. Weighs 12 pounds or more and measures 2½ feet long.

Snowshoe hare (or varying hare) — Occurs throughout Alaska except for lower portion of Alaska Peninsula, arctic coast, and most islands; scarce in Southeast. Cyclic population highs and lows of hares occur roughly every 10 years. Reddish brown color in summer, white in winter. Named for their big hind feet, covered with coarse hair in winter, which make for easy travel over snow.

Brown lemming — Found throughout northern Alaska and the Alaska Peninsula. Not present in Southeast, Southcentral or Kodiak archipelago. Cyclic population highs and lows.

Collared lemming — Found from Brooks Range north and from lower Kuskokwim River drainage north.

Northern bog lemming (sometimes called lemming mice) — Tiny mammals, rarely observed, occur in meadows and bogs across most of Alaska.

Deer mouse — Inhabit timber and brush in Southeast.

House mouse — Found in Alaska seaports and large communities in Southcentral.

BIRDS

Meadow jumping mouse — Found in southern third of Alaska from Alaska Range to Gulf of Alaska.

Collared pika — Found in central and southern Alaska; most common in Alaska Range.

Porcupine — Found in most wooded regions of mainland Alaska.

Raccoon — Not native to Alaska and considered an undesirable addition because of impact on native fur bearers. Found on west coast of Kodiak Island, and on Japonski and Baranof islands and other islands off Prince of Wales Island in Southeast.

Norway rat — Came to Alaska on whaling ships to Pribilof Islands in mid-1800s; great numbers of these rats thrived in the Aleutians (the Rat Islands group is named for the Norway rats). Found in virtually all Alaska seaports and in Anchorage and Fairbanks and other population centers with open garbage dumps.

Bushy-tailed woodrat — Found along mainland coast of Southeast. Commonly named pack rats, they carry off objects such as coins, buttons, or bits of broken glass, often leaving a stick or similar object in their place.

Shrews — Seven species range in Alaska.

Meadow vole (or meadow mouse) — Seven species attributed to Alaska range throughout the state.

Red-backed vole — Found throughout Alaska from Southeast to Norton Sound.

Woodchuck — Found in eastern Interior between Yukon and Tanana rivers, from east of Fairbanks to Alaska-Canada border. Large, burrowing squirrels, also called ground hogs.

Authorities at the University of Alaska acknowledge 405 species of birds in Alaska. If undocumented sightings are included, the number of species increases to more than 420. Although only about half the species are waterbirds, they are by far the most numerous birds in the state. Thousands of ducks, geese, and swans make their way north each spring to take advantage of Alaska's lakes, tundra ponds, and river flats. In addition, millions of pelagic birds (seabirds) congregate in great

nesting colonies on exposed sea cliffs along much of Alaska's coastline. Some of the best-known pelagic bird areas are in the Aleutian and Pribilof islands.

Migratory birds gather in Alaska from many corners of the world. The arctic tern travels up to 22,000 miles round trip each year from Antarctic waters to breed in Alaska. The lesser golden plover nests in Alaska and winters in Hawaii. Other species travel between Alaska and Asia.

The Copper River Delta, situated along one of the most important migration routes in the state, is relatively accessible to bird watchers via the Copper River Highway from Cordova. Each May, one of the world's largest concentrations of birdlife — primarily sandpipers and dunlins — funnels by the millions through the delta region. The delta is also an important waterfowl breeding area, containing the world's only breeding population of dusky Canada geese. Approximately four-fifths of the world's population of trumpeter swans nests in Alaska. Although the swans were once thought near extinction, about 8,000 were counted in 1980.

Other important waterfowl nesting areas include the great delta between the mouths of the Yukon and Kuskokwim rivers, Yukon Flats, Innoko Flats, and Minto Lakes. Additional gathering spots during migrations include Egegik, Port Heiden, Port Moller, Izembek Bay, Chickaloon Flats, Susitna Flats and Stikine Flats. A few species of birds — including shearwaters, albatross, and petrels — breed in Antarctic waters and winter in Alaska during the Northern Hemisphere's summer.

Four species of endangered birds are found in Alaska: the Aleutian Canada goose, the American and arctic races of peregrine falcon, the Eskimo curlew, and the short-tailed albatross.

Four chapters of the National Audubon Society are based in Alaska: the Anchorage Audubon Society (P.O. Box 1161, Anchorage 99510), the Juneau Audubon Society (P.O. Box 1725, Juneau 99802), the Kodiak Audubon Society (Box 1756, Kodiak 99615), and the Arctic Audubon Society (P.O. Box 60524, Fairbanks 99701). In addition to trying to help people increase their knowledge of birds and their surroundings, the groups (except for Fairbanks) coordinate an annual Christmas bird count. In Fairbanks, the Fairbanks Bird Club (P.O. Box 81791, Fairbanks 99708) conducts the annual Christmas bird count.

FACTS ABOUT ALASKA

ARCTIC CIRCLE

The Arctic Circle is the latitude at which the sun does not set for one day at midsummer and does not rise for one day at midwinter, when the sun is at its greatest distance from the celestial equator. The latitude, which varies slightly from year to year, is approximately 66°33′ from the equator.

On the day of summer solstice, on June 20 or 21, the sun does not set at the Arctic Circle; because of refraction of sunlight, it appears not to set for 4 days. Farther north, at Barrow (northernmost community in the United States), the sun does not set from May 10 to August 2.

At winter solstice, December 21 or 22, the sun does not rise for 1 day at the Arctic Circle. At Barrow, it does not rise for 67 days.

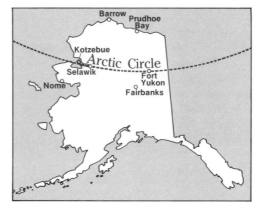

AURORA BOREALIS

The aurora borealis is produced by gas particles in the upper atmosphere being struck by solar electronics trapped in the earth's magnetic field. Color varies depending on how hard the gas particles are being struck and range from simple arcs to drapery-like forms in green, red, blue and purple. The lights occur in a pattern rather than as a solid glow because electric current sheets flowing through gases create V-shaped potential double layers. Electrons near the center of the current sheet move faster, hit the atmosphere harder, and cause the different intensities of light observed in the aurora.

Displays occur about 68 miles above the earth's surface, concentrated in two bands roughly centered above the Arctic Circle and Antarctic Circle. Greatest occurrence of auroral displays is in the spring and fall months, although displays may occur on dark nights throughout the winter.

Some observers claim the northern lights make a noise similar to the rustle of taffeta, but scientists say the displays cannot be heard in the audible frequency range.

To capture the northern lights on film, you will need a sturdy tripod, a locking-type cable release (some 35mm cameras have both *time* and *bulb* settings, but most have *bulb only*, which calls for use of the locking-type cable release), and a camera with a f/3.5 lens (or faster).

It is best to photograph the lights on a night when they are not moving too rapidly. And, as a general rule, photos improve if you manage to include recognizable subjects in the foreground—trees and lighted cabins being favorites of many photographers. Set your camera up at least 75 feet back from the foreground objects to make sure that both the foreground and aurora are in sharp focus.

Normal and wide-angle lenses are best. Try to keep your exposures under a minute—10 to 30 seconds are generally best. The following lens openings and exposure times are only a starting point, since the amount of light generated by the aurora is inconsistent. (It's best to bracket exposures widely for best results.)

	ASA 200	ASA 400
f1.2	3 sec.	2 sec.
f1.4	5	3
f1.8	7	4
f2	20	10
f2.8	40	20
f3.5	60	30

Ektachrome 200 and 400 color films can be push-processed in the home darkroom or by some custom-color labs, allowing use of higher ASA ratings (800, 1200 or even 1600 on the 400 ASA film, for example). Kodak will push-process film if you include an ESP-1 envelope with your standard film-processing mailer. (Consult your local camera store for details.)

A few notes of caution:

Protect the camera from low temperatures until you are ready to make your exposures. Some newer cameras, in particular, have electrically controlled shutters that will not function properly at low temperatures.

Wind the film slowly to reduce the possibility of static electricity, which can lead to streaks on the film. Grounding the camera when rewinding can help prevent the static-electricity problem. (To ground the camera, hold it against a water pipe, drain pipe, metal fence post or other grounded object.)

Follow the basic rules, experiment with exposures, and you should obtain good results.

BALEEN

Long, fringed, bonelike strips that line the mouth of baleen whales. Baleen strains out plankton, the tiny, shrimplike creatures called krill, and small fish from the water. Once used for corset stays and buggy whips, baleen is no longer used commercially, although Alaska Natives still use brownish black bowhead baleen to make baskets and model ships for the tourist trade.

BARABARA

Pronounced *buh-rah-buh-rah,* this traditional Aleut or Eskimo shelter is built of sod supported by driftwood or whalebone.

BOATING

Travel by boat is an important means of transportation in Alaska, where highways cover only about one-third of the state. Until the advent of the airplane, boats were often the only way to reach many parts of Alaska. Most of Alaska's supplies still arrive by water, and in Southeast — where precipitous terrain and numerous islands make road building impossible — water travel is essential.

There are approximately 36,000 vessels between 20 feet and 100 feet long registered in Alaska. Of these, approximately 6,200 are longer than 30 feet, and many are commercial fishing vessels.

To accommodate the needs of this fleet, there are approximately 7,000 slips available at public small-boat harbors in Alaska. According to the state, actual service capacity is somewhat greater because of the transient nature of many boats and certain management practices allowing "double parking." There are also harbors at various remote locations; no services other than moorage are provided at these harbors.

The Alaska Department of Transportation and Public Facilities (Pouch Z, Juneau 99811), through its regional offices, has the major responsibility for providing public floats, grids, docks, launching ramps, and associated small-boat harbor facilities throughout the coastal areas of the state. Often these facilities are leased to local governments at no cost. Moorage facilities constructed by the state are intended for boats up to a maximum of 100 feet, with a limited number of facilities for larger vessels where large boats are common. With the exception of Ketchikan, Sitka, and Juneau, there are no private marina facilities.

More and more, people are discovering the pleasures of motorboating, sailing, canoeing, rafting, kayaking and powering shallow-draft river boats through Alaska's vast water wilderness.

Recreational boating opportunities are too numerous and varied to mention all of them here; Alaska has thousands of miles of lakes, rivers, and sheltered seaways. For information on boating rivers, lakes, and seaways within national forests, parks, monuments, preserves, and wildlife refuges, contact the appropriate federal agency. For travel by boat in southeastern Alaska's sheltered seaways — or elsewhere in Alaska's coastal waters — NOAA nautical charts are available.

Canoe trails have been established on the Kenai Peninsula (contact the Kenai National Wildlife Refuge, P.O. Box 2139, Soldotna 99669); in Nancy Lake recreation area (contact the Superintendent, Mat-Su District, P.O. Box 182, Palmer 99645); and on rivers in the Fairbanks and Anchorage areas (contact the Bureau of Land Management, 701 C Street, Box 13, Anchorage 99513).

Travel by water in Alaska requires extra caution, however. Weather changes fast and is often unpredictable; it's important to be prepared for the worst. Alaska waters, even in midsummer, are cold; a person falling overboard may become immobilized by the cold water in only a few minutes. And since on many of Alaska's water routes one is so remote from civilization, help may be a long way off.

Persons inexperienced in traveling Alaska's waterways might consider employing a charter boat operator or outfitter. Guides offer local knowledge and provide all necessary equipment. The Division of Tourism (Pouch E, Juneau 99811) maintains current lists of such services. Another place to find names of guides and charter skippers is in The Guide Post® in *ALASKA*® magazine, available from Alaska Northwest Publishing Company.

CAMPING

Numerous public and privately operated campgrounds are found along Alaska's highways. Electrical hookups and dump stations are scarce. Alaska's back country offers virtually limitless possibilities for wilderness camping. Get permission before camping on private land. If the land is publicly owned, it's worthwhile to contact the agency that manages the land regarding regulations and hiking/camping conditions. Additional details about camping are found in *The MILEPOST ®*.

THE U.S. FOREST SERVICE maintains campgrounds in the Tongass (southeastern Alaska) and Chugach (southcentral Alaska) national forests, most with tent and trailer sites and minimum facilities. All campgrounds are available first-come, first-served; most are four dollars per night, a few are free, and some with more complete facilities are five dollars per night. Campgrounds are usually open from late May to early September. More information is available from the Forest Supervisor, Chugach National Forest, 2221 East Northern Lights Boulevard, Suite 230, Anchorage 99504, or the Forest Supervisor, Tongass National Forest, P.O. Box 1628, Juneau 99802.

THE NATIONAL PARK SERVICE (state office: 540 West Fifth Avenue, Anchorage 99501) at Denali National Park offers one walk-in and six campgrounds accessible by road; all are available on a first-come, first-served basis. Situated near the park entrance and open year-round are Riley Creek, for tents and trailers, and Morino, for walk-in tent campers. The others are open between May and September, depending on weather. Brochures may be obtained from Denali National Park, P.O. Box 9, Denali Park 99755.

Glacier Bay National Park and Katmai National Park each offer one campground for walk-in campers. Back-country camping is permitted in Denali, Glacier Bay, Katmai and Klondike Gold Rush parks, as well as the other national parks and monuments in Alaska.

ALASKA DIVISION OF PARKS (619 Warehouse Drive, Suite 210, Anchorage 99501) maintains the most extensive system of roadside campgrounds and waysides in Alaska. All are on a first-come, first-served basis. There are no fees.

U.S. FISH AND WILDLIFE SERVICE (state office: 1011 East Tudor, Anchorage 99503) has several wildlife refuges open to campers, although most are not accessible by highway. The Kenai National Wildlife Refuge, however, has several campgrounds accessible from the Sterling Highway linking Homer and Anchorage.

THE BUREAU OF LAND MANAGEMENT (BLM) maintains 25 campgrounds in interior Alaska. BLM campgrounds are free (except for the Delta BLM campground on the Alaska Highway). Write the Bureau of Land Management, 701 C Street, Box 13, Anchorage 99513.

COST OF LIVING

Cost of food, clothing, housing, and gasoline are 15 percent to 45 percent higher in Alaska than in the lower 48 states. The following chart shows unofficial sample costs in the spring of 1982.

	ANCHORAGE	FAIRBANKS	JUNEAU
Apartment rental, 1-bedroom	$275-$490	$389-$409	$430-$500
Apartment rental, 2-bedroom	$340-$700	$488-$536	$450-$700
Apartment rental, 3-bedroom	$375-$850	$688	$475-$800
Purchase 2-bedroom home	$78,000-$97,000	$79,000-$84,770	$60,000-$85,000
Purchase 3-bedroom home	$89,000-$167,000	$98,770-$114,000	$89,000-$131,000
Purchase 4-bedroom home	$118,000-$195,000	$113,818-$131,096	$94,000-$154,000
Firewood, per cord	$90-$125	$85-$100	
Gasoline, premium or unleaded, per gal. (full-serve & self-serve)	$1.49 & $1.38	$1.62 & $1.54	$1.45 & $1.31
Gasoline, regular, per gal. (full-serve & self-serve)	$1.45 & $1.29	$1.56 & $1.47	$1.34 & $1.25
Gasoline, diesel, per gal.	$1.17-$1.35	$1.42	$1.31
Car insurance (low risk, married adult over 25 driving medium-sized late model car), full coverage per year	$500-$600	$605	$208-$325
Auto tune-up, compact	$80-$100	$65-$100	$38-$45
Auto tune-up, V8	$110-$160	$85-$125	$46-$58
Heating oil, per gal.	$1.25	$1.20	
Milk, per qt.	$.81	$.85	$.83-$.87
Eggs, medium, per doz.	$.98	$1.05	$.94
Lettuce, per lb.	$.79-$.98	$.82	$.59-$.79
Bread, 24-oz. loaf	$.69-$1.14	$.69-$1	$1.23-$1.75
Ground beef, per lb.	$1.89	$1.63	$1.49-$2.19
Steak dinner (New York cut)	$8.50-$18	$9.50-$20	$14.95-$17.95
Coffee, per cup	$.40-$1	$.40	$.50-$1
Ham and eggs	$3.40-$6.75	$3.50-$4.50	$3.50-$4.75
Hamburger	$.75-$5.95	$3.50-$4.50	$2.85-$7.50

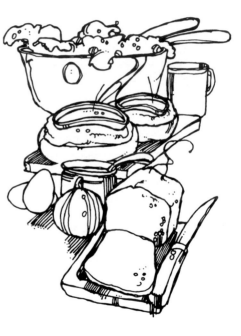

DAYLIGHT HOURS

Summer Maximum

	SUNRISE	SUNSET	HOURS OF DAYLIGHT
Barrow	May 10	August 2	84 days
Fairbanks	12:59 A.M.	10:48 P.M.	21:49 hours
Anchorage	2:21 A.M.	9:42 P.M.	19:21 hours
Juneau	3:51 A.M.	10:09 P.M.	18:18 hours
Ketchikan	4:04 A.M.	9:33 P.M.	17:29 hours
Adak	5:27 A.M.	10:10 P.M.	16:43 hours

Winter Minimum

	SUNRISE	SUNSET	HOURS OF DAYLIGHT
Barrow	Jan. 24 noon	Nov. 18 noon	none
Fairbanks	9:59 A.M.	1:41 P.M.	3:42 hours
Anchorage	9:14 A.M.	2:42 P.M.	5:28 hours
Juneau	9:46 A.M.	4:07 P.M.	6:21 hours
Ketchikan	9:12 A.M.	4:18 P.M.	7:06 hours
Adak	9:52 A.M.	5:38 P.M.	7:46 hours

DOG MUSHING

Sled dog racing is Alaska's official state sport. Races ranging from world championship class to local club meets are held throughout the winter.

The sprint or championship races are usually run over two or three days with the cumulative time for the heats deciding the winner. Distances for the heats vary from about 12 miles to 30 miles.

Alaska's most famous sled dog race is the Iditarod. The first race, conceived and organized by Joe Redington, Sr., of Knik, began in Anchorage on March 3, 1973, and ended April 3, 1973, in Nome. Of the 34 who started the race, 22 finished. The Iditarod has been run every year since its inception in 1973. In 1976 it was declared Alaska's official sled dog race by Gov. Jay Hammond. That year also, Congress designated the Iditarod as a National Historic Trail.

Following the old dog team mail route from Knik to Nome blazed in 1910, the trail crosses two mountain ranges, follows the Yukon River for about 150 miles, runs through several bush villages, and crosses the pack ice of Norton Sound.

Strictly a winter trail because the ground is mostly spongy muskeg swamps, the route attracted national attention in 1925 when sled dog mushers, including the famous Leonhard Seppala, relayed 300,000 units of life-saving diphtheria serum to epidemic-threatened Nome.

Each year the Iditarod takes a slightly different course, following an alternate southern route in odd years. While the route is traditionally described as 1,049 miles long (a figure that was selected because Alaska is the 49th state), actual distance is close to 1,200 miles.

Today, up to 50 mushers from all over the world come to Anchorage in March to run the world's longest — and richest — sled dog race. The Iditarod purse is divided among the first 20 finishers.

EARTHQUAKES

Between 1899 and May 1965 nine Alaska earthquakes occurred that equaled or exceeded a magnitude of 8 on the Richter scale. During the same period, more than 60 earthquakes took place that were of magnitude 7 or greater on the Richter scale.

According to the University of Alaska's Geophysical Institute, earthquake activity in Alaska typically follows the same pattern from month to month, interspersed with sporadic swarms, or groups of small earthquakes. The most active part of the state seismically is the Aleutian Islands arc system. Seismicity related to this system extends into interior Alaska to a point near Mount McKinley. These earthquakes are largely the result of underthrusting of the North Pacific plate and are characteristically deeper in the earth than most earthquakes. The majority of earthquakes resulting from this underthrusting occur in Cook Inlet —particularly near Mount Iliamna and Mount Redoubt — and near Mount McKinley. North of the Alaska Range, in the central Interior, most earthquakes are of shallow origin.

An earthquake created the highest splash wave ever recorded when, on the evening of July 9, 1958, a quake with a magnitude of 8 on the Richter scale rocked the Yakutat area. A landslide containing approximately 40 million cubic yards of rock plunged into Gilbert Inlet at the head of Lituya Bay. The gigantic splash resulting from the slide sent a wave 1,740 feet up the opposite mountain side, denuding it of trees and soil down to bedrock. It then fell back and swept through the length of the bay and out to sea. One fishing boat anchored in Lituya Bay at the time was lost with its crew of two; another was carried over a spit of land by the wave and soon after foundered, but its crew was saved. A third boat anchored in the bay miraculously survived intact. A total of four square miles of coniferous forest was destroyed.

The most destructive earthquake to strike Alaska occurred at 5:36 P.M. on Good Friday, March 27, 1964. Registering between 8.4 and 8.6 on the Richter scale, the earthquake was the strongest ever recorded in North America. With its primary epicenter deep beneath Miners Lake in northern Prince William Sound, the earthquake spread shock waves over a 500-mile-wide area. The earthquake and seismic waves that followed killed 131 persons, 115 of them Alaskans. The death tally was: Anchorage, 9; Chenega, 23; Kodiak, 19; Point Nowell, 1; Point Whitshed, 1; Port Ashton, 1; Port Nellic Juan, 3; Seward, 13; Valdez, 31; Whittier, 13.

The 1964 earthquake — referred to as Black Friday — released twice the energy of the San Francisco earthquake of 1906 and moved more earth farther, both horizontally and vertically, than any other earthquake ever recorded. In the 69-day period after the main quake, there were 12,000 jolts of 3.5 magnitude or greater.

The highest seismic sea wave ever recorded was caused by the 1964 earthquake when an undersea slide near Shoup Glacier in Port Valdez triggered a wave that toppled trees 100 feet above tidewater and deposited silt and sand 220 feet above salt water.

FIRES, FOREST AND TUNDRA

The largest single fire ever recorded in Alaska burned 1,161,200 acres 74 miles northwest of Galena in 1957, according to Bureau of Land Management figures. In 1977, the Bear Creek fire, largest in the United States that year, consumed 361,000 acres near the Farewell airstrip.

CALENDAR YEAR	NO. OF FIRES	ACRES BURNED
1955	190	23,582
1956	226	476,593
1957	391	5,049,661
1958	278	317,215
1959	320	596,574
1960	238	87,180
1961	117	5,100
1962	102	38,975
1963	194	16,290
1964	164	3,430
1965	148	7,093
1966	256	672,765
1967	207	109,005
1968	442	1,013,301
1969	511	4,231,820
1970	487	113,486
1971	472	1,069,108
1972	641	963,686
1973	336	59,816
1974	782	662,960
1975	344	127,845
1976	622	69,119
1977	681	2,209,408
1978	356	7,757
1979	620	432,425
1980	417	188,778
1981	556	758,335

FLAG

Alaska's state flag was designed in 1926 by Benny Benson, who entered his design in a territorial flag contest for schoolchildren. The Alaska legislature adopted his design as the official flag of the Territory of Alaska on May 2, 1927. The flag consists of eight gold stars on a field of blue — the Big Dipper and the North Star. In Benson's words: "The blue field is for the Alaska sky and the forget-me-not, an Alaska flower. The North Star is for the future state of Alaska, the most northerly of the Union. The dipper is for the Great Bear —symbolizing strength."

Benny Benson was born October 12, 1913, at Chignik, Alaska. His mother was of Aleut-Russian descent and his father was a Swedish fisherman who came to the Alaska Territory in 1904. Benson's mother died of pneumonia when Benny was four, and he entered the Jesse Lee Memorial Home (then located at Unalaska).

The territorial flag contest was open to all Alaska schoolchildren in grades 7 through 12. Benny, then a seventh grade student at the Jesse Lee Home, was one of 142 students whose designs were selected for the final judging by a committee chosen by the Alaska Department of the American Legion.

Benny was awarded a $1,000 scholarship and was presented an engraved watch for winning the contest. He used the scholarship

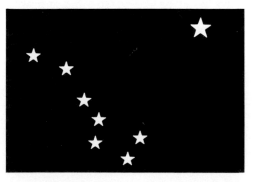

to attend the Hemphill Engineering School in Seattle in 1937. In 1963, the Alaska legislature awarded Benson an additional $2,500 as a way "of paying a small tribute to a fellow Alaskan." In November of the same year, Benson presented his award watch to the Alaska State Museum.

Benny's prophetic words, "The North Star is for the future state of Alaska, the most northerly of the Union," were realized on January 3, 1959, when Alaska was proclaimed the 49th state of the Union. The drafters of the Constitution for Alaska stipulated that the flag of the territory would be the official flag of the state of Alaska, and when the flag was first flown over the capital city on July 4, 1959, Benny proudly led the parade that preceded the ceremony, carrying the flag of "eight stars on a field of blue," which he had designed many years before.

Benson returned to Alaska in 1949, settling in Kodiak where he worked as a mechanic for Kodiak Airways. He was active in a movement to integrate the Elks, a white-only national organization which now has a number of Native members in Alaska. Benson had a leg amputated in 1969 and his health declined; he died of a heart attack on July 2, 1972, in Kodiak.

In 1981, the Alaska legislature appropriated $25,000 for a monument to Benson, at the intersection of Benson Boulevard and Minnesota Drive in Anchorage. The bowl-shaped aluminum sculpture (six feet by four feet, on a nine-foot concrete base) by artist Gerald Conoway of Anchorage features spokes representing the stars of the Alaska flag.

There is also a memorial to Benny Benson on the Seward Highway just outside Seward.

FOREST SERVICE CABINS

There are 177 U.S. Forest Service public-use recreational cabins available for $10 per party (no limit) per night in Alaska. Tongass National Forest in southeastern Alaska has 142 cabins and Chugach National Forest in southcentral Alaska has 35 cabins.

Most of the cabins are accessible only by plane or boat, a few by hiking trail. Average cabin size is 12 by 14 feet. Most cabins have wood stoves, some have oil stoves. All cabins have tables and sleeping room for six people. You must supply bedding, cookware, stove oil and food. Firewood may be obtained at the site from dead and downed trees. There are pit toilets but no garbage dumps. Skiffs are provided at some cabins.

Cabins must be reserved in person or by mail. Advance reservations can be made up to 180 days prior to use. You must have a permit for the specific length of occupancy. There is a seven-day use limit; three-day limit May to August on hike-in cabins.

For cabin reservations and information, contact the U.S. Forest Service, Tongass National Forest, Box 1628, Juneau 99802, Chugach National Forest, 2221 E. Northern Lights Boulevard, Suite 230, Anchorage, 99504; or stop by the district ranger offices in Cordova, Ketchikan, Seward, Sitka, and Petersburg.

GOLD NUGGETS

The largest gold nugget ever found in Alaska was discovered near Nome. The nugget, weighing 107 ounces, 2 pennyweight, was found September 29, 1901, on Discovery Claim, Anvil Creek, Nome District. The nugget was 7 inches long, 4 inches wide and 2 inches thick.

Two other record-breaking nuggets were found in the Nome area the same month. On September 5, the largest Alaska nugget found up to that time was discovered on the Jarvis Brothers' claim on Anvil Creek. It weighed 45 ounces, and was 6¼ inches long, 3¼ inches wide, 1⅜ inches thick at one end and ½ inch thick at the other. On September 14, a larger nugget was found on the Discovery Claim; it weighed 97 ounces and broke the record of September 5 only to be superseded by the 107-ounce nugget found on the 29th.

GOLD STRIKES AND RUSHES

1848	First Alaska gold discovery (Russian on Kenai Peninsula)
1861	Stikine River near Telegraph Creek, British Columbia
1872	Cassiar district in Canada (Stikine headwaters country)
1872	Near Sitka
1874	Windham Bay near Juneau
1880	Gold Creek at Juneau
1886	Fortymile discovery
1887	Yakutat beach areas and Lituya Bay
1893	Mastodon Creek, starting Circle City
1895	Sunrise district on Kenai Peninsula
1896	Klondike strike, Bonanza Creek, Canada
1898	Anvil Creek, Nome
1898	Atlin district, British Columbia
1900	Porcupine rush out of Haines
1902	Fairbanks (Felix Pedro, Pedro Dome)
1906	Innoko
1907	Ruby
1908	Iditarod
1913	Marshall
1913	Chisana
1914	Livengood

GOVERNORS OF ALASKA

Under Russia

Emperor Paul of Russia grants the Russian-American Company an exclusive trade charter in Alaska.

Chief Managers, Russian-American Company	
Alexander Andreevich Baranof	1799-1818
Leontil Andreanovich Hagemeister	January-October 1818
Semen Ivanovich Yanovski	1818-1820
Matxei I. Muravief	1820-1825
Peter Egorovich Chistiakov	1825-1830
Baron Ferdinand P. vonWrangell	1830-1835
Ivan Antonovich Kupreanof	1835-1840
Adolph Karlovich Etolin	1840-1845
Michael D. Tebenkof	1845-1850
Nikolai Y. Rosenberg	1850-1853
Alexander Ilich Rudakof	1853-1854
Stephen Vasili Voevodski	1854-1859
Ivan V. Furuhelm	1859-1863
Prince Dmitri Maksoutoff	1863-1867

Under United States

U.S. purchases Alaska from Russia in 1867; U.S. Army given jurisdiction over Department of Alaska.

Army Commanding Officers	
Brevet Maj. Gen. Jefferson C. Davis	October 18, 1867-August 31, 1870
Brevet Lt. Col. George K. Brady	September 1, 1870-September 22, 1870
Maj. John C. Tidball	September 23, 1870-September 19, 1871
Maj. Harvey A. Allen	September 20, 1871-January 3, 1873
Maj. Joseph Stewart	January 4, 1873-April 20, 1874
Capt. George R. Rodney	April 21, 1874-August 16, 1874
Capt. Joseph B. Campbell	August 17, 1874-June 14, 1876
(Captain E. Field was in command for one month during 1875 while Captain Campbell was out of Alaska.)	
Capt. John Mendenhall	June 15, 1876-March 4, 1877
Capt. Arthur Morris	March 5, 1877-June 14, 1877

U.S. Army troops leave Alaska; the highest ranking federal official left in Alaska is the U.S. Collector of Customs. Department of Alaska is put under control of the U.S. Treasury Department.

U.S. Collectors of Customs	
Montgomery P. Berry	June 14, 1877-August 13, 1877
H.C. DeAhna	August 14, 1877-March 26, 1878
Mottrom D. Ball	March 27, 1877-June 13, 1879

U.S. Navy is given jurisdiction over the Department of Alaska.

Navy Commanding Officers	
Captain L.A. Beardslee	June 14, 1879-September 12, 1880
Comdr. Henry Glass	September 13, 1880-August 9, 1881
Comdr. Edward P. Lull	August 10, 1881-October 18, 1881
Comdr. Henry Glass	October 19, 1881-March 12, 1882
Comdr. Frederick Pearson	March 13, 1882-October 3, 1882
Comdr. Edgar C. Merriman	October 4, 1882-September 13, 1884
Lt. Comdr. Henry E. Nichols	September 14, 1884-September 15, 1884

Alaska becomes a state January 3, 1959.

Elected Governors	
William A. Egan (Elected)	January 3, 1959-December 5, 1966
Walter J. Hickel (Elected-resigned)	December 5, 1966-January 29, 1969
Keith H. Miller (Succeeded)	January 29, 1969-December 5, 1970
William A. Egan (Elected)	December 5, 1970-December 5, 1974
Jay S. Hammond (Elected)	December 5, 1974-December 5, 1982
William J. Sheffield (Elected)	December 5, 1982-

Congress provides civil government for the new District of Alaska in 1884; on August 24, 1912, territorial status is given to Alaska.

Presidential Appointments

John H. Kinkead (President Arthur) (He did not reach Sitka until September 15, 1884)	July 4, 1884-May 7, 1885
Alfred P. Swineford (President Cleveland)	May 7, 1885-April 20, 1889
Lyman E. Knapp (President Harrison)	April 20, 1889-June 18, 1893
James Sheakley (President Cleveland)	June 18, 1893-June 23, 1897
John G. Brady (President McKinley)	June 23, 1897-March 2, 1906

Presidential Appointments (continued)

Wilford B. Hoggatt (President Roosevelt)	March 2, 1906-May 20, 1909
Walter E. Clark (President Taft)	May 20, 1909-April 18, 1913
John F.A. Strong (President Wilson)	April 18, 1913-April 12, 1918
Thomas Riggs, Jr. (President Wilson)	April 12, 1918-June 16, 1921
Scott C. Bone (President Harding)	June 16, 1921-August 16, 1925
George A. Parks (President Coolidge)	June 16, 1925-April 19, 1933
John W. Troy (President Roosevelt)	April 19, 1933-December 6, 1939
Ernest Gruening (President Roosevelt)	December 6, 1939-April 10, 1953
B. Frank Heintzleman (President Eisenhower)	April 10, 1953-January 3, 1957
Mike Stepovich (President Eisenhower)	April 8, 1957-August 9, 1958

Delegates to Congress

In 1906, Congress authorized Alaska to send a voteless delegate to the House of Representatives.

Frank H. Waskey	1906-1907
Thomas Cale	1907-1909
James Wickersham	1909-1917
Charles A. Sulzer	1917-contested election
James Wickersham	1918-seated as delegate
Charles A. Sulzer	1919-elected; died before taking office
George Grigsby	1919-elected in a special election
James Wickersham	1921-seated as delegate, having contested election of Grigsby
Dan A. Sutherland	1921-1930
James Wickersham	1931-1933

Delegates to Congress (continued)

Anthony J. Dimond	1933-1944
E. L. Bartlett	1944-1958

Unofficial delegates to Congress to promote statehood, elected under a plan first devised by Tennessee when it was seeking statehood. The Tennessee Plan Delegates were not seated by Congress but did serve as lobbyists.

Senators:	
Ernest Gruening	1956-1958
William A. Egan	1956-1958
Representative:	
Ralph Rivers	1956-1958

Alaska becomes 49th state in 1959. Alaska sends two senators and one representative to U.S. Congress.

Senators:	
E. L. Bartlett	1959-1968
Ernest Gruening	1959-1968
Mike Gravel	1968-1980
Ted Stevens	1968-
Frank Murkowski	1981-
Representatives:	
Ralph Rivers	1959-1966
Howard Pollock	1966-1970
Nicholas Begich	1970-1972
Don Young	1973-

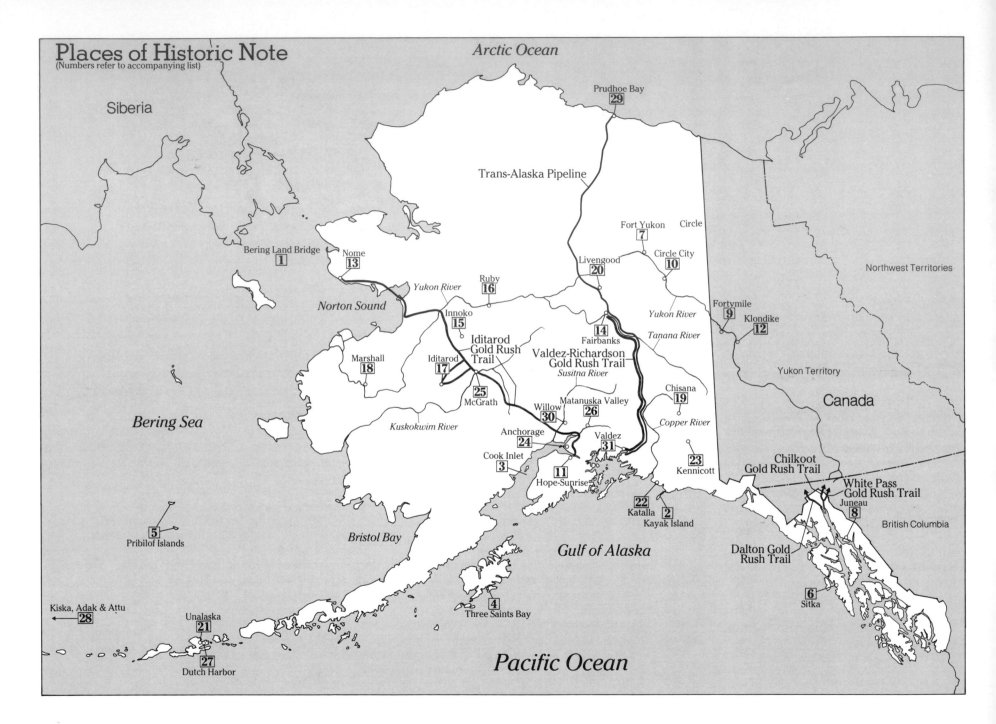

Places of Historic Note
(Numbers refer to accompanying list)

Arctic Ocean

Siberia

Prudhoe Bay
29

Trans-Alaska Pipeline

Bering Land Bridge
1

Nome
13

Fort Yukon
7

Circle

Livengood
20

Circle City
10

Northwest Territories

Ruby
16

Yukon River

Norton Sound

Innoko
15

Fortymile
9

Klondike
12

Yukon River

Tanana River

14

Fairbanks

Iditarod Gold Rush Trail

Marshall
18

Iditarod
17

Valdez-Richardson Gold Rush Trail

Susitna River

Yukon Territory

25

McGrath

30
Willow

Matanuska Valley
26

Chisana
19

Canada

Bering Sea

Kuskokwim River

Anchorage
24

Valdez
31

Copper River

23
Kennicott

Chilkoot Gold Rush Trail

Cook Inlet

3

11

Hope-Sunrise

White Pass Gold Rush Trail

Juneau
8

5
Pribilof Islands

Bristol Bay

Gulf of Alaska

22
Katalla

2
Kayak Island

British Columbia

Dalton Gold Rush Trail

Kiska, Adak & Attu
28

Unalaska
21

4
Three Saints Bay

6
Sitka

Dutch Harbor
27

Pacific Ocean

HISTORY

Numbers refer to accompanying map on facing page.

6,000-11,000 years ago — Human culture in southeastern, Aleutians, interior, and northwest arctic Alaska.

6,000 years ago — Most recent migration from Siberia across the land bridge (1).

3,000-5,000 years ago — Human culture on the Bering Sea coast.

200-300 years ago — Tlingits and Haidas arrive.

1725 — Vitus Bering sent by Peter the Great to explore the North Pacific.

1741 — On a later expedition, Bering in one ship and Alexei Chirikof in another discover Alaska. Chirikof, according to ship logs, probably sees land on July 15 a day ahead of his leader, who was perhaps 300 miles or more to the north of him. Georg Steller goes ashore on Kayak Island, becoming the first white man known to have set foot on Alaska soil (2).

1743 — Russians begin concentrated hunting of sea otter, continuing until the species is almost decimated; fur seal hunting begins later.

1774-1794 — Explorations of Alaska waters by Juan Perez, James Cook (3) and George Vancouver.

1784 — First Russian settlement in Alaska, at Three Saints Bay, Kodiak Island (4).

1786 — Russians discover the Pribilof Islands (5), later to resettle Aleuts to the formerly uninhabited islands for fur sealing.

1794 — Vancouver sights Mount McKinley.

1799 — Alexander Baranof establishes the Russian post known today as Old Sitka (6); a trade charter is granted to the Russian-American Company.

1821 — Foreign vessels prohibited from trade in Alaska waters, making the Russian-American Company the sole trading firm.

1824-1842 — Russian exploration of the mainland leads to discovery of the Kuskokwim, Nushagak, Yukon and Koyukuk rivers.

1847 — Fort Yukon established by Hudson's Bay Company (7).

1848 — First mining in Alaska, on the Kenai Peninsula.

1853 — Russian explorers-trappers find the first oil seeps in Cook Inlet.

1857 — Coal mining begins at Coal Harbor, Kenai Peninsula, to supply steamers.

1859 — Baron Edoard de Stoeckl, minister and charge d'affaires of the Russian delegation to the United States, is given authority to negotiate the sale of Alaska.

1867 — United States buys Alaska from Russia for $7.2 million; treaty signed March 30, formal transfer takes place on October 18 at Sitka. Fur seal population begins to stabilize. U.S. Army is given jurisdiction over the Department of Alaska the following year.

1872 — Gold discovered near Sitka (6). Later discoveries include Juneau, 1874, 1880 (8); Fortymile, 1886 (9); Circle City, 1893 (10); Sunrise District (Kenai Peninsula), 1895 (11); Klondike, 1896 (12); Nome, 1898 (13); Fairbanks, 1902 (14); Innoko, 1906 (15); Ruby, 1907 (16); Iditarod, 1908 (17); Marshall, 1913 (18); Chisana, 1913 (19); and Livengood, 1914 (20).

1878 — First salmon canneries at Klawock and Old Sitka.

1887 — Tsimshians, under Father William Duncan, arrive at Metlakatla from British Columbia.

1891 — First oil claims staked in Cook Inlet area. First Siberian reindeer brought to Unalaska by Sheldon Jackson.

1897-1900 — Klondike gold rush in Yukon; heavy traffic through Alaska.

1902 — First oil production, at Katalla (22); telegraph from Eagle to Valdez completed.

1906 — Peak gold production year; Alaska granted a nonvoting delegate to Congress.

1911 — Copper production begins at Kennicott (23).

1912 — Territorial status for Alaska; first territorial legislature is convened the following year.

1913 — First airplane flight in Alaska, at Fairbanks.

1914 — Anchorage founded as a work camp for the Alaska Railroad (24).

1916 — First bill proposing Alaska statehood introduced in Congress; peak copper production year.

1922 — First pulp mill starts production, Speel River, near Juneau.

1923 — President Warren Harding drives spike completing the Alaska Railroad.

1924 — Carl Ben Eielson lands at McGrath with the first air mail delivery in Alaska (25).

1935 — Matanuska Valley Project begins, which establishes farming families in Alaska (26). First Juneau to Fairbanks flight.

1936 — All-time record salmon catch in Alaska — 126.4 million fish.

1940 — Military build-up in Alaska; Fort Richardson, Elmendorf Air Force Base established. At this point there are only about 40,000 non-Native Alaskans and 32,458 Natives. Pan American Airways inaugurates twice-weekly service between Seattle, Ketchikan and Juneau, using Sikorsky flying boats.

1942 — Dutch Harbor bombed (27) and Attu and Kiska islands occupied by Japanese forces (28). Alaska Highway built; first overland connection to Lower 48.

1943 — Japanese forces driven from Alaska.

1944 — Alaska-Juneau Mine shuts down.

1953 — Oil well drilled near Eureka, on the Glenn Highway, marking the start of modern oil history; first plywood mill at Juneau; first big pulp mill at Ketchikan.

1957 — Kenai oil strike.

1958 — Statehood measure passed by Congress; statehood proclaimed officially January 3, 1959. Sitka pulp mill opens.

1964 — Good Friday earthquake, March 27, causes heavy damage throughout the Gulf Coast region; 131 people lost their lives.

1967 — Alaska Centennial celebration; Fairbanks flood.

1968 — Oil and gas discoveries at Prudhoe Bay on the North Slope (29); excitement begins. $900 million North Slope oil lease sale the following year; pipeline proposal follows.

1971 — Congress approves Alaska Native Land Claims Settlement Act, granting title to 40 million acres of land and providing more than $900 million in payment to Alaska Natives.

1974 — Trans-Alaska pipeline receives final approval; construction build-up begins.

1975 — Population and labor force soar with construction of pipeline; Alaska Gross

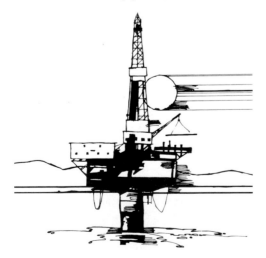

Products hits $5.8 billion — double the 1973 figure.

1976 — Voters select Willow area (30) for new capital site.

1977 — Completion of the trans-Alaska pipeline from Prudhoe Bay to Valdez; shipment of first oil by tanker from Valdez to Puget Sound.

1978 — 200-mile fishing limit goes into effect; President Jimmy Carter withdraws 56 million acres creating 17 new national monuments as of December 1, 1978.

1979 — State of Alaska files suit to halt the withdrawal of 56 million acres of Alaska land by President Carter under the Antiquities Act.

1980 — Special session of the Alaska legislature votes to repeal the state income tax and provides for refunds of 1979 taxes. Legislature establishes a Permanent Fund as a repository for one-fourth of all royalty oil revenues for future generations. Census figures show Alaska's population grew by 32.4 percent during the 1970s. The Alaska Lands Act of 1980 puts 53.7 million Alaska acres into the national wildlife refuge system, parts of 25 rivers to the national wild and scenic rivers system, 3.3 million acres to national forest lands, and 43.6 million acres to national park land.

1981 — Legislature puts on the ballot a constitutional amendment proposal to limit state spending. Secretary of the Interior James Watt initiates plans to sell oil and gas leases on 130 million acres of Alaska's nonrestricted federal land and announces a tentative schedule to open 16 offshore areas of Alaska as part of an intense national search for oil and gas on the outer continental shelf.

1982 — Oil revenues for state decrease. Funding of capital move from Juneau to Willow defeated in November election.

HOLIDAYS

New Year's Day	January 1
Lincoln's Birthday	February 12
Washington's Birthday	Third Monday in February
Seward's Day	Last Monday in March
Memorial Day	Last Monday in May
Independence Day	July 4
Labor Day	First Monday in September
Alaska Day	October 18
Veterans Day	November 11
Thanksgiving Day	Fourth Thursday in November
Christmas Day	December 25

Seward's Day commemorates the signing of the treaty by which the United States bought Alaska from Russia, signed on March 30, 1867. Alaska Day is the anniversary of the formal transfer of the territory and the raising of the U.S. flag at Sitka on that date in 1867.

HUNTING AND SPORT FISHING

There are 11 sport fishing and 20 game management units in Alaska. Information on current regulations for hunting and fishing in Alaska are available from the Department of Fish and Game, Box 3-2000, Juneau 99802. Hunting and fishing licenses, required for residents and nonresidents alike, are available at Fish and Game offices and sporting goods stores throughout the state.

Following are lists of sport fish species and trophy fish and game.

SPORT FISH SPECIES	BEST BAIT, LURE	MAXIMUM SIZE (lbs.)
Arctic char	spoon, eggs	20
Arctic grayling	flies	5
Brook trout	eggs, spin	5
Burbot	bait	30
Chum salmon	spoon	15
Cutthroat trout	bait, spin, flies	7
Dolly Varden	bait, spin, flies	15
Halibut	octopus, herring	300
King salmon	herring	100
Kokanee	spin, eggs	2
Lake trout	spoon, plug	45
Lingcod	herring	80
Northern pike	spoon, spin	30
Pink salmon	small spoon	10
Rainbow trout	flies, lures, bait	20
Red salmon	flies	15
Rockfish	herring, spin	20
Sheefish	spoon	50
Silver salmon	herring, spoon	25
Steelhead trout	spoon, eggs	45
Whitefish	flies, eggs	10

Trophy Fish

The following were recorded as record fish by the Alaska Department of Fish and Game since the establishment of the Trophy Fish Award program in 1964.

Arctic char/Dolly Varden: 17 pounds, 8 ounces; 36 inches; Wulik River, 1968; Peter Winslow.

Arctic grayling: 4 pounds, 11 ounces, 21½ inches; Ugashik Narrows, 1975; Duane Weaver.

Burbot: 24 pounds, 12 ounces; 43 inches; Lake Louise, 1976; George Howard.

Chum salmon: 27 pounds, 3 ounces; 39⅜ inches; Behm Canal, 1977; Robert Jahnke.

Cutthroat trout: 8 pounds, 6 ounces; 26¼ inches; Wilson Lake, 1977; Robert Denison.

Halibut: 440 pounds; 97½ inches; Point Adolphus, 1978; Joar Savland.

King salmon: 93 pounds; 50 inches; Kelp Bay, 1977; Howard Rider.

Kokanee: 2 pounds; 21¼ inches; Lake Lucile, 1977; James E. Gum, Jr.

Lake trout: 47 pounds; 44¼ inches; Clarence Lake, 1970; Daniel Thorness.

Northern pike: 38 pounds; 48 inches; Fish Creek, 15 miles east of Tanana, 1978; Rhonda Edward.

Pink salmon: 12 pounds, 9 ounces; 30 inches; Moose River, 1974; Steven Lee.

Rainbow/steelhead: 42 pounds, 2 ounces; 43 inches; Bell Island, 1970; David White.

Red salmon: 16 pounds; 31 inches; Kenai River, 1974; Chuck Leach.

Sheefish: 52 pounds, 8 ounces; 48 inches; Kobuk River, 1968; Jim Keeline.

Silver salmon: 26 pounds; 35 inches; Icy Strait, 1976; Andrew A. Robbins.

Whitefish: 7 pounds, 2 ounces; 25½ inches; Tolovana River, 1978; Glen W. Cornwall.

Trophy Game

Record big game as recorded by the Boone and Crockett Club are as follows:

Black bear: skull $13\frac{7}{16}$ inches long, $8\frac{6}{16}$ inches wide (1966).

Brown bear (coastal region): skull $17\frac{15}{16}$ inches long, $12\frac{13}{16}$ inches wide (1952).

Grizzly bear (inland): skull $16\frac{10}{16}$ inches long, $9\frac{14}{16}$ inches wide (1970).

Polar bear: skull $18\frac{8}{16}$ inches long, $11\frac{7}{16}$ inches wide (1963). It is currently illegal for anyone but an Alaskan Eskimo, Aleut, or Indian to hunt polar bear.

Bison: right horn $20\frac{4}{8}$ inches long, base circumference $14\frac{7}{8}$ inches; left horn $20\frac{4}{8}$ inches long, base circumference $15\frac{4}{8}$ inches; greatest spread $31\frac{6}{8}$ inches (1965).

Barren Ground caribou: right beam $51\frac{2}{8}$ inches, 22 points; left beam $51\frac{5}{8}$ inches, 23 points (1967).

Moose: right palm length $46\frac{3}{8}$ inches, width 17 inches; left palm length 51 inches, width $29\frac{6}{8}$ inches; right beam 18 points, left 17 points; greatest spread $77\frac{4}{8}$ inches (taken using an airplane in 1961).

Mountain goat: right horn $11\frac{5}{8}$ inches long, base circumference $5\frac{6}{8}$ inches; left horn $11\frac{5}{8}$ inches long, base circumference $5\frac{5}{8}$ inches (1933).

Musk ox: right horn $26\frac{6}{8}$ inches, left horn $26\frac{4}{8}$ inches, tip-to-tip spread $26\frac{7}{8}$ inches (1976).

Dall sheep: right horn $48\frac{5}{8}$ inches long, base circumference $14\frac{5}{8}$ inches; left horn $47\frac{7}{8}$ inches long, base circumference $14\frac{6}{8}$ inches (1961).

ICEBERGS

Icebergs are formed in Alaska wherever glaciers reach salt water or a freshwater lake. Some accessible places to view icebergs include Glacier Bay, Icy Bay, Yakutat Bay, Taku Inlet, Endicott Arm, portions of northern Prince William Sound (College Fiord, Barry Arm, Columbia Bay), Mendenhall Lake, and Portage Lake.

If icebergs contain little or no sediment, approximately 75 percent to 80 percent of their bulk may be underwater. The more sediment an iceberg contains, the greater its density; an iceberg containing large amounts of sediment may even float slightly beneath the surface. Glaciologists of the U.S. Geological Survey believe that some of these "black icebergs" may actually sink to the bottom of a body of water. Since salt water near the faces of glaciers may be liquid to temperatures as low as 28° F, and icebergs melt at 32° F, some of these underwater icebergs may remain unmelted indefinitely.

Alaska's icebergs are comparatively small compared to the icebergs found near Antarctica and Greenland. One of the largest icebergs ever recorded in Alaska was formed in May 1977 in Icy Bay. Glaciologists measured it at 346 feet long, 297 feet wide, and 99 feet above the surface of the water.

ICE, SEA

Sea water generally freezes at minus 2° C or 29° F. Most salt is leached out of sea ice. Ice closest to shore is called shorefast or landfast ice. It attaches itself to shore as freezing begins in fall and slowly builds seaward. Shorefast and other first-year ice may reach thicknesses of up to six feet. According to James L. Wise, state climatologist for Arctic and Environmental Information Data Center, the mean first-year ice line generally extends farthest south between February and March, following a line that runs approximately from Port Heiden to the Pribilofs, then northwest toward the Siberian coast. During cold winters, it may reach as far south as Cape Sarichef. Chukchi Sea ice generally lasts 6 to 7 months each year; ice covers the Beaufort Sea approximately 9 to 10 months per year.

Permanent pack ice generally occurs north of 72° north latitude. Some pack ice may reach thicknesses of 30 feet, though 6 to 12 feet is more common. Currents and winds move pack ice, resulting in leads, or open areas of water. Pressure ridges form between the moving pack ice and shorefast ice. Thicknesses of ice in these ridges may reach 10 to 20 feet above the surface of the water and several times that thickness below the surface.

In 1969 the National Weather Service began a low-profile sea ice reconnaissance program, which expanded greatly during the summer of 1975, when during a year of severe ice, millions of dollars of material had to be shipped to Prudhoe Bay. In 1976, headquarters for a seven-day-a-week ice watch was established at Fairbanks and then moved to Anchorage in 1981.

The National Weather Service operates a radio facsimile broadcast service making current ice analysis charts, special oceanographic charts, and standard weather charts available to the public via standard radios equipped with "black box" receivers. Commercial fishing operators, particularly in the Bering Sea, use the radio-transmitted charts to steer clear of problem weather and troublesome ice formations. More information is available from the National Weather Service in Kodiak or Anchorage.

ICEWORM

Although generally regarded as a hoax, iceworms actually exist. Small, thin, segmented black worms, usually less than one inch long, thrive at temperatures just above freezing. Observers as far back as the 1880s report that at dawn, dusk, or on overcast days, the tiny worms, all belonging to the genus *Mesenchytraeus,* may literally carpet the surface of glaciers. When sunlight strikes them, they burrow back down into the ice.

The town of Cordova commemorates its own version of the iceworm each February in the Iceworm Festival, when a 150-foot-long, multilegged "iceworm" marches in a parade down Main Street.

IGLOO

In Alaska, this dwelling is traditionally made of driftwood, whalebone, and sod. It was the Canadian Eskimos, not those of Alaska, who built the well-known houses of snow and ice. Alaska Natives, however, did sometimes build temporary shelters and storehouses of snow.

INFORMATION SOURCES

Agriculture: State Division of Agriculture, Pouch A, Wasilla 99687; Cooperative Extension Service, University of Alaska, Fairbanks 99701.

Alaska Natives: Alaska Federation of Natives Inc., 411 W. 4th Avenue, Suite 1-A, Anchorage 99501.

Boating, Canoeing, and Kayaking: U.S. Fish and Wildlife Service, 1011 E. Tudor, Anchorage 99503; Alaska Department of Natural Resources, Division of Parks, 619 Warehouse Avenue, Suite 210, Anchorage 99501.

Business: Alaska Department of Commerce and Economic Development, Division of Economic Enterprise, Pouch D, Juneau 99801; State Chamber of Commerce, 310 Second Street, Juneau 99801. A 60-page booklet titled *Establishing a Business in Alaska* may be obtained from the Division of Economic Enterprise.

Camping and Hiking: Alaska Department of Natural Resources, Division of Parks, 619 Warehouse Avenue, Suite 210, Anchorage 99501; Bureau of Land Management, 701 C Street, Box 13, Anchorage 99513; Alaska Department of Commerce and Economic Development, Division of Tourism, Pouch E, Juneau 99811; Supervisor, Chugach National Forest, 2221 E. Northern Lights Boulevard, Suite 230, Anchorage 99504; National Park Service, 540 W Fifth Avenue, Suite 202, Anchorage 99501, Supervisor, Tongass National Forest, P.O. Box 1628, Juneau 99802.

Census Data: Alaska Department of Labor, Research and Analysis Division, P.O. Box 1149, Juneau 99811.

Education: Alaska Department of Education, Pouch F, Juneau 99811; U.S. Bureau of Indian Affairs, Box 3-8000, Juneau 99802.

Gold Panning: Alaska Department of Natural Resources, Division of Geological and Geophysical Surveys, Mining Information, 323 E. Fourth Avenue, Pouch 7-005, Anchorage 99510; Bureau of Land Management, 701 C Street, Box 13, Anchorage 99513.

Health: Alaska Department of Health and Social Services, Pouch H-01, Juneau 99811.

Housing: Alaska State Housing Authority, Box 80, Anchorage 99510.

Hunting and Fishing Regulations: Department of Fish and Game, P.O. Box 3-2000, Juneau 99802.

Job Opportunities: State Employment Service, Box 3-7000, Juneau 99811.

Labor: Alaska Department of Labor, Box 1149, Juneau 99811.

Land: Division of Lands, Pouch 7-005, Anchorage 99510; Bureau of Land Management, 701 C Street, Box 13, Anchorage 99513.

Mines and Petroleum: State Division of Geological and Geophysical Surveys, 3001 Porcupine Drive, Anchorage 99501; Mines Information Office, 230 S. Franklin Street, Juneau 99801; Alaska Miners Association, Inc., 509 W. Third Avenue, Suite 17, Anchorage 99501; Alaska Oil and Gas Association, 505 W. Northern Lights Boulevard, Anchorage 99503.

River Running: National Park Service, 540 W. Fifth Avenue, Suite 202, Anchorage 99501; Alaska Association of Mountain and Wilderness Guides, 300 K Street, Suite 246, Australaska Building, Anchorage 99501.

Travel and Visitor Information: Division of Tourism, Pouch E, Juneau 99811; Marine Highway Systems, Pouch R, Juneau 99811.

IVORY

Eskimos traditionally carved ivory to make such implements as harpoon heads, dolls and *ulu* handles. For the past 80 years, however, most carvings have been made to be sold. The bulk of the ivory used today comes from walrus tusks and teeth. Fossil ivory is also used; it may be black, dark brown or beige, depending on the moisture conditions and soil in which it is found. Etching originally was done with hand tools and the scratches were filled in with soot. Today modern power tools supplement the hand tools and carvers color the etching with India ink. The most active carvers live on Saint Lawrence Island, the Seward Peninsula and Little Diomede Island.

Walrus may only be taken by Alaska Natives (Aleuts, Eskimos, and Indians) who dwell on the coast of the North Pacific Ocean or the Arctic Ocean for subsistence purposes or for the creation and sale of authentic Native articles of handicrafts or clothing.

Raw walrus ivory or other parts can only be sold by an Alaska Native to an Alaska Native within Alaska or to a registered agent for resale or transfer to an Alaska Native within the state. Only authentic Native processed ivory articles may be sold or transferred to a non-Native, or sold in interstate commerce.

Beach ivory, which is found on the beach within one-fourth mile of the ocean, may, however, be kept by anyone. This ivory must be registered by all non-Natives with the U.S. Fish and Wildlife Service or the National Marine Fisheries Service within 30 days of discovery. Beach-found ivory must remain in the possession of the finder even if carved or scrimshawed.

Carved or scrimshawed walrus ivory (authentic Native handicraft) or other marine mammal parts made into clothing or other authentic Native handicrafts may be exported from the United States to a foreign country, but the exporter must first obtain an export permit from the U.S. Fish and Wildlife Service. Importation of walrus or other marine mammals is illegal except for scientific research purposes or for public display once a permit is granted.

For further information contact: Special Agent-in-Charge, U.S. Fish and Wildlife Service, 1011 East Tudor Road, Anchorage 99503, phone (907) 263-3311; or Senior Resident, U.S. Fish and Wildlife Service, 1412 Airport Way, Fairbanks 99701, phone (907) 456-4839.

JADE

Most Alaskan jade is found near the Dall, Shungnak, and Kobuk rivers and Jade Mountain, all north of the Arctic Circle. The stones occur in various shades of green, brown, black, yellow, white, and even red. The most valuable are those that are marbled black, white, and green. Gem-quality jade, about one-fourth of the total mined, is used in jewelry making. Fractured jade is used for clock faces, table tops, book ends, and other items. Jade is the Alaska state gem.

LANGUAGES

Besides English, Alaska's languages include Haida, Tlingit, Tsimshian, Aleut, several dialects of Eskimo, and several dialects of Athabascan.

MOSQUITOES

Twenty-five species of mosquitoes are found in Alaska, the females of all species feeding on people, other mammals or birds. Males *and* females eat plant sugar, but only the females suck blood, which they use for egg production. No Alaska mosquitoes carry diseases. The insects are present from April through September in many areas of the state. From Cook Inlet south, they concentrate on coastal flats and forested valleys. In the Aleutian Islands, mosquitoes are absent or present

only in small numbers. The most serious mosquito infestations occur in moist areas of fields, bogs, and forests of interior Alaska, from Bristol Bay eastward. Mosquitoes are most active at dusk and dawn; low temperatures and high winds decrease their activity. Mosquitoes may be controlled by draining their breeding areas or spraying with approved insecticides. When traveling in areas of heavy mosquito infestations, it is wise to wear protective clothing, carefully screen living and camping areas, and use a good insect repellent.

NATIONAL FORESTS

Alaska's two national forests, the Tongass in Southeast, and the Chugach in Southcentral, are the nation's largest and second-largest national forests respectively. The Alaska National Interest Lands Conservation Act of 1980 — also referred to as the Alaska d-2 lands bill or lands act — increased the acreage and changed the status of certain lands in Alaska's national forests.

The Alaska d-2 lands bill created approximately 5.3 million acres of wilderness (consisting of 14 units) within the 16-million-acre Tongass National Forest. It also added three new areas to the forest: the Juneau Icefield, Kates Needle, and parts of the Brabazon Range, totaling more than 1 million acres.

The lands bill also provided extensive additions to the Chugach National Forest. These additions, totaling about 2 million acres, include the Nellie Juan area east of Seward, College Fiord extension, Copper/Rude rivers addition, and a small extension at Controller Bay southeast of Cordova.

The following charts show the effect of the Alaska lands act on the Tongass and Chugach national forests.

	TONGASS	CHUGACH
Total acreage before act	15,555,388	4,392,646
Total acreage after act	16,954,713	5,940,040*
Wilderness acreage created	5,361,899 acres**	none created
Wilderness Study	none created	2,019,999 acres
Wild and Scenic River Study	Situk River***	none created

* The lands act provides for additional transfers of national forest land to Native Corporations, the state, and the Fish and Wildlife Service of an estimated 296,000 acres on Afognak Island and an estimated 242,000 acres to the Chugach Native Corporation.
** Final acreage may vary from these figures as official boundary maps are completed.
*** The lands act provides for a maximum of 640 acres on each side of the river, for each mile of river length.

NEW WILDERNESS UNITS IN TONGASS NATIONAL FOREST	ACRES
Admiralty Island National Monument*	900,000
Coronation Island Wilderness	19,122
Endicott River Wilderness	94,000
Maurelle Islands Wilderness	4,424
Misty Fiords National Monument*	2,136,000
Petersburg Creek-Duncan Salt Chuck Wilderness	50,000
Russell Fiord Wilderness	307,000
South Baranof Wilderness	314,000
South Prince of Wales Wilderness	97,000
Stikine-LeConte Wilderness	443,000
Tebenkof Bay Wilderness	65,000
Tracy Arm-Fords Terror Wilderness	656,000
Warren Island Wilderness	11,353
West Chichagof-Yakobi Wilderness	265,000
Total Acreage	5,361,899**

* Designated monuments under d-2 bill; first areas so designated in the National Forest system.
** The final acreage of wilderness areas may vary from these figures as official boundary maps are completed and state and Native selection acreages are deleted from these totals.

NATIONAL PARKS, PRESERVES AND MONUMENTS

The National Park Service administers approximately 51.2 million acres of land in Alaska, consisting of 13 units classified as national parks, national preserves, and national monuments. The Alaska National Interest Lands Conservation Act of 1980 — also referred to as the Alaska d-2 lands bill or lands act — created 10 new National Park Service units in Alaska and changed the size and status of the three existing park service units: Mount McKinley National Park, now Denali National Park and Preserve; Glacier Bay National Monument, now a national park and preserve; and Katmai National Monument, now a national park and preserve. See map on page 178.

National parks are traditionally managed to preserve scenic, wildlife, and recreational values; mining, logging, hunting, and other resource exploitation are usually not permitted within park boundaries and motorized access is restricted to automobile traffic on authorized roads. However, regulations for National Park Service units in Alaska recognize that these units contain lands traditionally occupied and used by Alaska Natives and rural residents for subsistence activities. Therefore, management of all parks, preserves, and monuments in Alaska provide for subsistence hunting, fishing, and gathering activities, and the use of such motorized vehicles as snow machines, motorboats, and airplanes, where such activities are customary. In addition, the national preserves permit sport hunting.

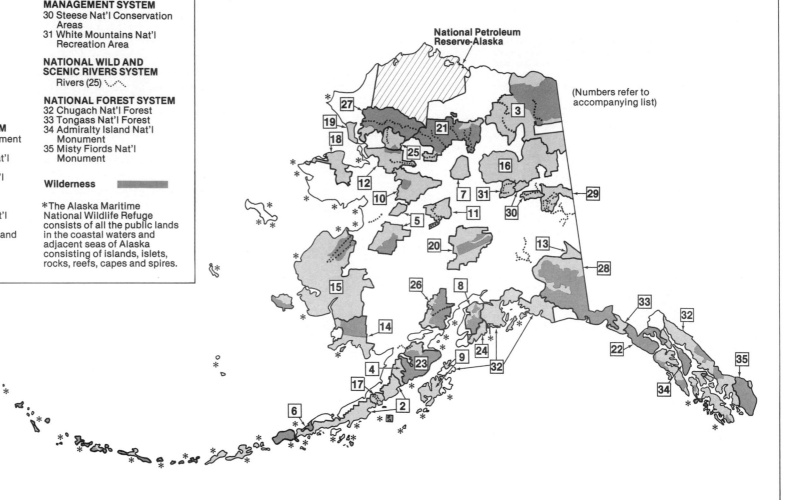

Alaska National Interest Lands

NATIONAL WILDLIFE REFUGE SYSTEM
1 Alaska Maritime NWR*
  a Chukchi Sea Unit
  b Bering Sea Unit
  c Aleutian Island Unit
  d Alaska Peninsula Unit
  e Gulf of Alaska Unit
2 Alaska Peninsula
3 Arctic
4 Becharof
5 Innoko
6 Izembek
7 Kanuti
8 Kenai
9 Kodiak
10 Koyukuk
11 Nowitna
12 Selawik
13 Tetlin
14 Togiak
15 Yukon Delta
16 Yukon Flats

NATIONAL PARK SYSTEM
17 Aniakchak Nat'l Monument and Preserve
18 Bering Land Bridge Nat'l Preserve
19 Cape Krusenstern Nat'l Monument
20 Denali Nat'l Park and Preserve
21 Gates of the Arctic Nat'l Park and Preserve
22 Glacier Bay Nat'l Park and Preserve
23 Katmai Nat'l Park and Preserve

24 Kenai Fjords Nat'l Park
25 Kobuk Valley Nat'l Park
26 Lake Clark Nat'l Park and Preserve
27 Noatak Nat'l Preserve
28 Wrangell Saint Elias Nat'l Park and Preserve
29 Yukon Charley Rivers Nat'l Preserve

BUREAU OF LAND MANAGEMENT SYSTEM
30 Steese Nat'l Conservation Areas
31 White Mountains Nat'l Recreation Area

NATIONAL WILD AND SCENIC RIVERS SYSTEM
Rivers (25)

NATIONAL FOREST SYSTEM
32 Chugach Nat'l Forest
33 Tongass Nat'l Forest
34 Admiralty Island Nat'l Monument
35 Misty Fiords Nat'l Monument

Wilderness

*The Alaska Maritime National Wildlife Refuge consists of all the public lands in the coastal waters and adjacent seas of Alaska consisting of islands, islets, rocks, reefs, capes and spires.

National Petroleum Reserve-Alaska

(Numbers refer to accompanying list)

NATIONAL PARK SERVICE UNITS	ACREAGE, MAJOR FEATURES, RECREATION
Aniakchak National Monument and Preserve Superintendent, Katmai National Park and Preserve Box 7, King Salmon 99613	514,000 acres Aniakchak caldera
Bering Land Bridge National Preserve National Park Service Nome 99762	2,457,000 acres Lava fields, archaeological sites, migratory waterfowl
Cape Krusenstern National Monument National Park Service Kotzebue 99752	560,000 acres Archaeological sites
Denali National Park and Preserve National Park Service McKinley Park 99755	5,696,000 acres Mount McKinley, abundant wildlife
Gates of the Arctic National Park and Preserve National Park Service Fairbanks 99701	7,952,000 acres Brooks Range, wild and scenic rivers, wildlife
Glacier Bay National Park and Preserve National Park Service P.O. Box 1089, Juneau 99802	3,328,000 acres Glaciers, marine wildlife
Katmai National Park and Preserve National Park Service P.O. Box 7, King Salmon 99613	4,268,000 acres Valley of Ten Thousand Smokes, brown bears
Kenai Fjords National Park National Park Service 540 West Fifth Avenue, Anchorage 99501	567,000 acres Fjords, Harding Icefield
Kobuk Valley National Park National Park Service 540 West Fifth Avenue, Anchorage 99501	1,710,000 acres Archaeological sites, Great Kobuk Sand Dunes, river rafting
Lake Clark National Park and Preserve National Park Service 540 West Fifth Avenue, Anchorage 99501	3,653,000 acres Back-country recreation, fishing, scenery
Noatak National Preserve National Park Service 540 West Fifth Avenue, Anchorage 99501	6,460,000 acres River floating, abundant wildlife
Wrangell-Saint Elias National Park and Preserve National Park Service P.O. Box 29, Glennallen 99588	12,318,000 acres Rugged, peaks, glaciers, expansive wilderness
Yukon-Charley Rivers National Preserve National Park Service Eagle 99738	1,713,000 acres Back-country recreation, river floating

NATIONAL WILD AND SCENIC RIVERS

The Alaska National Interest Lands Conservation Act of December 2, 1980, gave wild and scenic river classification to 13 streams within the National Park System, 6 in the National Wildlife Refuge System, and 2 in Bureau of Land Management Conservation and Recreation areas. The remaining 5 rivers are located outside designated preservation units. Twelve more rivers were designated for further study and possible wild and scenic classification.

The criteria for wild and scenic river classification are not just for its float trip possibilities. Scenic features, wilderness characteristics and other recreational opportunities that would be impaired by alteration, development or impoundment are also considered.

Rivers are classified into three categories under the Wild and Scenic Rivers Act. The wild classification is most restrictive of development or incompatible uses — it stresses the wilderness aspect of the rivers. The scenic classification permits some intrusions upon the natural landscape, and recreational classification is the least restrictive category. A specified amount of land back from the river's banks is also put in protected status to ensure access, use, and the preservation of aesthetic values for the public.

For those desiring to float these rivers, special consideration must be given to put-in and take-out points as most of the new wild and scenic rivers are not accessible by road. This means that voyagers and their crafts have to be flown in and picked up by charter bush planes. Because Federal Aviation Administration regulations prohibit the lashing of canoes and kayaks on pontoons of floatplanes when carrying passengers, inflatable rafts and folding canvas or rubber kayaks are often more convenient and less expensive to transport.

RIVERS WITHIN NATIONAL PARK AREAS

Alagnak	Katmai National Preserve
Alatna	Gates of the Arctic National Park
Aniakchak	Aniakchak National Monument and Preserve
Charley	Yukon-Charley Rivers National Preserve
Chilikadrotna	Lake Clark National Park and Preserve
John	Gates of the Arctic National Park and Preserve
Kobuk	Gates of the Arctic National Park and Preserve
Mulchatna	Lake Clark National Park and Preserve
Noatak	Gates of the Arctic National Park and Noatak National Preserve
North Fork Koyukuk	Gates of the Arctic National Park and Preserve
Salmon	Kobuk Valley National Park
Tinayguk	Gates of the Arctic National Park and Preserve
Tlikakila	Lake Clark National Park

RIVERS WITHIN NATIONAL WILDLIFE REFUGES

Andreafsky	Yukon Delta National Wildlife Refuge
Ivishak	Arctic National Wildlife Refuge
Nowitna	Nowitna National Wildlife Refuge
Selawik	Selawik National Wildlife Refuge
Sheenjek	Arctic National Wildlife Refuge
Wind	Arctic National Wildlife Refuge

RIVERS WITHIN BUREAU OF LAND MANAGEMENT UNITS

Beaver Creek — The segment of the main stem from confluence of Bear and Champion creeks within White Mountains National Recreation Area and Yukon Flats National Wildlife Refuge.

Birch Creek — The segment of the main stem from the south side of Steese Highway downstream to approximately Twelvemile House on Steese Highway, within Steese National Conservation Area.

RIVERS OUTSIDE OF DESIGNATED PRESERVATION UNITS

Alagnak — Those segments or portions of the main stem and Nonvianuk tributary lying outside and westward of Katmai National Park and Preserve.

Delta River — The segment from and including all of the Tangle Lakes to a point one-half mile north of Black Rapids.

Fortymile River — The main stem within the state of Alaska, plus tributaries.

Gulkana River — The main stem from the outlet of Paxson Lake to the confluence with Sourdough Creek; various segments of the west fork and middle fork.

Unalakleet River — Approximately 65 miles of the main stem.

RIVERS DESIGNATED FOR STUDY FOR INCLUSION IN WILD AND SCENIC RIVER SYSTEM

Colville River	Porcupine River
Etivluk-Nigu Rivers	Sheenjek River (lower segment)
Kanektok River	Situk River
Kisaralik River	Squirrel River
Koyuk River	Utukok River
Melozitna River	Yukon River (Ramparts section)

Further information on rivers and river running can be obtained from offices of the National Park Service, 540 West Fifth Avenue, Anchorage 99501; the U.S. Fish and Wildlife Service, 1011 East Tudor Road, Anchorage 99503; and the Bureau of Land Management, P.O. Box 13, Anchorage, 99513.

NATIONAL WILDERNESS AREAS

Passage of the Alaska National Interest Lands Conservation Act, on December 2, 1980, added millions of acres to the National Wilderness Preservation System. Administration of these wilderness areas is the responsibility of the agency under whose jurisdiction the land is situated. Agencies which administer wilderness areas in Alaska include the National Park Service, U.S. Fish and Wildlife Service, and the U.S. Forest Service. Although the Bureau of Land Management (BLM) has authority to manage wilderness in the public domain, no BLM wilderness areas exist in Alaska.

Wilderness allocations to different agencies in Alaska are:

AGENCY	APPROXIMATE ACREAGE
U.S. Forest Service	5,360,000
National Park Service	32,355,000
U.S. Fish and Wildlife Service	18,560,000

Wilderness, according to the Wilderness Act of 1964, is land sufficient in size to enable the operation of natural systems without undue influence from activities in surrounding areas, and should be places in which man himself is a visitor who does not remain. Alaska wilderness regulations follow the stipulations of the Wilderness Act as amended by the Alaska lands act. Specifically designed to allow for Alaska conditions, the rules are considerably more lenient about transportation access, man-made structures, and use of mechanized vehicles. The primary objective of a wilderness area continues to be the maintenance of the wilderness character of the land. In Alaska wilderness areas, the following uses and activities are permitted:

- Fishing, hunting and trapping will continue on lands within the national forests, national wildlife refuges, and national park preserves. National park wilderness does not allow these activities.
- Subsistence uses, including hunting, fishing, trapping, berry gathering, and use of timber for cabins and firewood will be permitted in wilderness areas by all agencies.
- Public recreation cabins in wilderness areas in national forests, national wildlife refuges, and national park preserves will continue to be maintained and may be replaced. A limited number of new public cabins may be added if needed.
- Existing special use permits and leases on all national forest wilderness lands for cabins, homesites or similar structures will continue. Use of temporary campsites, shelters, and other temporary facilities and equipment related to hunting and fishing on national forest lands will continue.
- Fish habitat enhancement programs, including construction of buildings, fish weirs, fishways, spawning channels, and other accepted means of maintaining, enhancing, and rehabilitating fish stocks will be allowed in national forest wilderness areas. Reasonable access including use of motorized equipment will be permitted.
- Special use permits for guides and outfitters operating within wilderness areas in the national forests will be allowed to continue.
- Private, state, and Native lands surrounded by wilderness areas will be guaranteed access through the wilderness area.
- Use of airplanes, motorboats, and snow machines where *traditional* as a means of access into wilderness areas will be allowed to continue.

NATIONAL WILDLIFE REFUGES

There are approximately 76 million acres of National Wildlife Refuge lands in Alaska administered by the U.S. Fish and Wildlife Service. (National wildlife refuge acreage in Alaska increased nearly fourfold with the signing of the Alaska d-2 lands bill — Alaska National Interest Lands Conservation Act — in December 1980.) Wildlife refuges are designed to protect the habitats of representative populations of land and marine mammals, other marine animals, and birds. Thus the 16 refuges vary widely in size, depending upon the life cycles and habitat requirements of a particular species. See map on page 178.

Among the public recreational uses permitted within national wildlife refuges are sightseeing, nature observation and photography, sport hunting and fishing, boating, camping, hiking, and picnicking. Trapping can be carried out under applicable state and federal laws. Commercial fishing, including use of motorized vehicles, is allowed.

Subsistence living activities within national wildlife refuges are all protected under the d-2 lands bill. Use of snowmobiles, motorboats and other means of surface transportation traditionally relied upon by local rural residents for subsistence is generally permitted. Aircraft access to wildlife refuges is allowed, and off-road vehicles may be used on special routes and in areas designated by the refuge manager.

NATIONAL WILDLIFE REFUGE ADMINISTRATIVE OFFICES	ACREAGE AND MAJOR FEATURES
Alaska Maritime National Wildlife Refuge Operations Manager South 1011 East Tudor Road Anchorage 99503	3,548,956 acres Seabirds, sea lions, sea otters, harbor seals
Alaska Peninsula National Wildlife Refuge Operations Manager South 1011 East Tudor Road Anchorage 99503	3,500,000 acres Brown bears, caribou, moose, sea otters, bald eagles, peregrine falcons
Arctic National Wildlife Refuge Refuge Manager Room 226, Federal Building & Courthouse, 101 12th Avenue Fairbanks 99701	18,054,624 acres Caribou, polar bears, grizzly bears, wolves, Dall sheep, peregrine falcons
Becharof National Wildlife Refuge Refuge Manager P.O. Box 211, King Salmon 99613	1,200,000 acres Brown bears, bald eagles
Innoko National Wildlife Refuge Operations Manager North 1011 East Tudor Road Anchorage 99503	3,850,000 acres Migratory birds, beavers
Izembek National Wildlife Refuge Refuge Manager Pouch 2, Cold Bay 99571	320,893 acres Black brant, brown bears
Kanuti National Wildlife Refuge Operations Manager North 1011 East Tudor Road Anchorage 99503	1,430,000 acres Migratory waterbirds, fur bearers, moose
Kenai National Wildlife Refuge Refuge Manager Box 2139, Soldotna 99669	1,970,000 acres Moose, salmon, mountain goats, Dall sheep, bears
Kodiak National Wildlife Refuge Refuge Manager Box 825, Kodiak 99615	1,865,000 acres Brown bears

NATIONAL WILDLIFE REFUGE ADMINISTRATIVE OFFICES	ACREAGE AND MAJOR FEATURES
Koyukuk National Wildlife Refuge Operations Manager North 1011 East Tudor Road Anchorage 99503	3,550,000 acres Wolves, caribou
Nowitna National Wildlife Refuge Operations Manager North 1011 East Tudor Road Anchorage 99503	1,560,000 acres Migratory waterfowl, caribou, moose, bears, fur bearers
Selawik National Wildlife Refuge Operations Manager North 1011 East Tudor Road Anchorage 99503	2,150,000 acres Migratory waterbirds
Tetlin National Wildlife Refuge Operations Manager North 1011 East Tudor Road Anchorage 99503	700,000 acres Migratory waterfowl, Dall sheep
Togiak National Wildlife Refuge Operations Manager South 1011 East Tudor Road Anchorage 99503	4,105,000 acres Nearly every major wildlife species of Alaska is represented
Yukon Delta National Wildlife Refuge Refuge Manager Box 346, Bethel 99559	19,624,458 acres Migratory birds, musk ox are found on Nunivak Island
Yukon Flats National Wildlife Refuge Refuge Manager Room 226, Federal Building & Courthouse, 101 12th Avenue Fairbanks 99701	8,630,000 acres Waterfowl

NATIVE PEOPLE

Of Alaska's Native people, who make up 16 percent of the state's total population, roughly 40,000 are Eskimos, 25,000 are Indians, and 7,000 are Aleuts. Many live in widely separated villages along the coastline and great rivers of the state. The village, rather than the tribe, is the unit; the Alaska tribe is the language group. Natives are migrating to the cities; about 5,000 live in Fairbanks, 10,000 in Anchorage.

At the time of European discovery in 1741, the Eskimo, Indian, and Aleut peoples lived within well-defined regions, and there was little mixing of ethnic groups. In Southeast, the salmon, deer, and other plentiful foods permitted the Tlingit, Tsimshian, and Haida Indians to settle in permanent villages and develop a culture rich in art. The Athabascan Indians of the Interior followed the migrating caribou and took advantage of seasonal abundance of fish, waterfowl, and other game. The Eskimos and Aleuts, like the Tlingits, depended on the sea.

The Tsimshians migrated in 1887 from their former home in British Columbia to Annette Island, under Anglican minister Father William Duncan. About 1,000 now live in Metlakatla and cooperatively run a salmon cannery, four fish traps, a water system, a hydroelectric plant, and a logging industry. Like most southeastern people, they are primarily fishermen.

Between 700 and 800 Haidas live in Alaska, about 200 of whom live in Hydaburg on the south end of Prince of Wales Island. They emigrated from Canada in the 1700s; more than 1,100 live in the Queen Charlotte Islands. Haidas excelled in the art of totem carving and are noted for fine slate carvings and precise and delicate working of wood, bone, and shell.

About 10,000 to 12,000 Tlingits are well distributed in southeastern Alaska; another 1,000 live in other areas of the state, primarily in the Anchorage area. Tlingits, who arrived from Canada before the first European contact, commercially dominated the interior Canadian Indians, trading eulachon oil, copper pieces, and Chilkat blankets for various furs. Like the Haidas, they are part of the totem culture that has attracted so much attention in southeastern Alaska. The totems provided a historic record of major events in the life of a family or clan.

The Athabascans, before European contact, were nomadic. There was no agriculture. They are closely related to the Navajos and Apaches of southwestern United States. The approximately 7,000 Athabascans all speak similar languages.

The Aleuts have traditionally lived on the Alaska Peninsula, eastward to the Ugashik River on the north and to Pavlof Bay on the south, extending down the Aleutian Chain and nearby islands. When the Russians reached the Aleutians in the 1740s, there were an estimated 16,000 to 20,000 Aleuts and practically every island was inhabited, but now only a few have permanent Aleut settlements. Some live on the Pribilof Islands, where they work for the U.S. government in handling the seal herds.

The Aleuts lived in permanent villages, taking advantage of sea life and land mammals for food. The original houses were large, communal structures, partly buried; later houses were small, single-family units. Today they live in frame houses, and many are commercial fishermen. Their language is related to the Eskimo, but far removed. The Aleuts are divided into two groups speaking slightly different dialects.

The Eskimos have traditionally lived in villages along the harsh Bering Sea and Arctic Ocean coastlines, and extended southward along the Gulf of Alaska coast. They took salmon, waterfowl, berries, ptarmigan, and a few caribou, but it was in sea and ice hunting that they excelled. Whales, seals, and walrus were the mainstay of their economy. Houses were partly buried and covered with sod; they did not build snow igloos.

Rapid advances in communications, transportation, and other services to remote villages, along with economic changes, have altered Native lifestyles in much of Alaska. A change from subsistence economy to money economy in some areas has largely been brought about by the passage of the Alaska Native Land Claims Settlement Act. Passed by Congress in 1971, the act gave Alaska Natives $962.5 million and 40 million acres of land as compensation for the loss of lands historically occupied by the Natives of Alaska.

Native Regional Corporations

Twelve regional business corporations were formed under the 1971 Alaska Native Land

STATE PARK SYSTEM

Claims Settlement Act to manage money and land received from the government. (A 13th corporation was organized for those Natives residing outside Alaska.) Following is a list of corporations and the area or region each administers:

Ahtna Incorporated (Copper River Basin), Drawer G, Copper Center 99573 or 1577 C Street, Suite 256, Anchorage 99501.

Aleut Corporation (Aleutian Islands), 2550 Denali, Suite 900, Anchorage 99503.

Arctic Slope Regional Corporation (Arctic Alaska), P.O. Box 129, Barrow 99723.

Bering Straits Native Corporation (Seward Peninsula), P.O. 1008, Nome 99762 or P.O. Box 3396, Anchorage 99510.

Bristol Bay Native Corporation (Bristol Bay area), P.O. Box 198, Dillingham 99576 or P.O. Box 220, Anchorage 99510.

Calista Corporation (Yukon-Kuskokwim Delta), P.O. Box 648, Bethel 99559 or 516 Denali Street, Anchorage 99501.

Chugach Natives, Inc. (Prince William Sound), 903 W. Northern Lights Boulevard, Suite 201, Anchorage 99503.

Cook Inlet Region, Inc. (Cook Inlet region), 2525 C Street, P.O. Drawer 4-N, Anchorage 99509.

Doyon Limited (interior Alaska), 201 First Avenue, Fairbanks 99701.

Koniag, Inc. (Kodiak area), P.O. Box 746, Kodiak 99615.

NANA Regional Corporation, Inc. (Kobuk region), P.O. Box 49, Kotzebue 99752 or 4706 Harding Drive, Anchorage 99503.

Sealaska Corporation (southeastern Alaska), One Sealaska Plaza, Suite 400, Juneau 99801.

The 13th Regional Corporation (outside Alaska), 1800 Westlake Avenue N., Suite 313, Seattle, WA 98109.

The Alaska state park system began in July 1959 with the transfer of federally-managed campgrounds and recreation sites from the Bureau of Land Management to the new state of Alaska. These sites were managed by the state Division of Lands until 1970; under the Forestry, Parks and Recreation Section until 1966; then under the Parks and Recreation Section. The Division of Parks was created in October 1970.

The Alaska state park system consists of 82 individual units divided into 7 park management districts. There are 56 recreation sites, 11 recreation areas, 4 historic parks, 3 historic sites, 3 state trails, and 5 state parks (Chugach, Denali, Chilkat, Kachemak Bay, and Wood-Tikchik). In addition there are the following state-owned park facilities under non-state management: Chilkoot Trail, 13 acres, Skagway, managed by the National Park Service; Totem Square, 0.5 acre, Ketchikan, managed by the Pioneers' Home; and Valdez Glacier Wayside, 226 acres, Valdez, managed by the City of Valdez.

Campsites are available on a first-come, first-served basis. In addition to camping and picnicking, many units offer hiking trails and boat launching ramps; most developed campgrounds have picnic tables and toilets. General information on the state park system is available from the Division of Parks, 619 Warehouse Avenue, Suite 210, Anchorage 99501.

The state park units are listed by park management district below and on the following pages. Designations for units of the Alaska state park system are abbreviated as follows: SP-State Park, SHP-State Historic Park, SHS-State Historic Site, SRA-State Recreation Area, SRS-State Recreation Site, ST-State Trail. Park units designated "undeveloped" may have camping, hiking trails, and limited facilities. Parks which indicate no developed campsites or picnic sites may offer fishing or river access, hiking and other activities. Numbers in the list refer to the map on page 185.

MAP KEY	ACREAGE	CAMP-SITES	PICNIC SITES	NEAREST TOWN
SOUTHEAST DISTRICT Box 142 Sitka 99835				
1 Baranof Hill SHS	1			Sitka
2 Chilkat SP	6,045	32	15	Haines
3 Chilkoot Lake SRS	80	32		Haines
4 Halibut Point SRS	40		9	Sitka
5 Juneau ST	15			Juneau
6 Mosquito Lake SRS	5	13		Haines
7 Old Sitka SHS	51			Sitka
8 Portage Cove SRS	7	9	3	Haines
9 Refuge Cove SRS	13		14	Ketchikan
10 Totem Bight SHP	11			Ketchikan

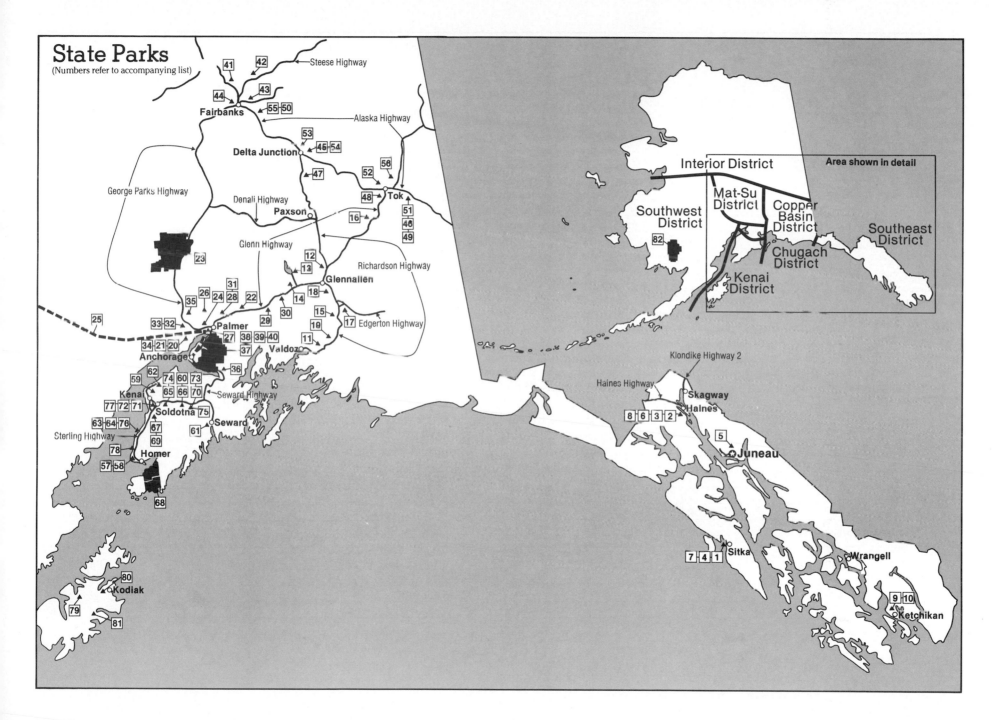

State Parks
(Numbers refer to accompanying list)

41 42 ← Steese Highway
44 43
55 50
Fairbanks
Alaska Highway
53
46 54
Delta Junction
56
47 52
George Parks Highway
48 Tok
Denali Highway 51
Paxson 46
49
Glenn Highway 16
12
23 13
Glennallen
Richardson Highway
31 18
26 24 28 22 14
35 30 15
25 29 17 Edgerton Highway
33 32 Palmer 10
34 21 20 27 38 39 40 11
Anchorage 37 Valdez
36
62
59 74 60 73
65 66 70
Kenai Seward Highway
77 72 71 Soldotna 75
63 64 76 Seward
Sterling Highway 67 61
69
78 Homer
57 58
68

80
Kodiak
79
81

Interior District
Area shown in detail
Mat-Su District
Copper Basin District
Southwest District
Southeast District
Chugach District
82
Kenai District

Klondike Highway 2
Haines Highway
Skagway
Haines
8 6 3 2
5
Juneau

Sitka
7 4 1
Wrangell

9 10
Ketchikan

COPPER BASIN DISTRICT
P.O. Box 286
Glennallen 99588

MAP KEY	ACREAGE	CAMP-SITES	PICNIC SITES	NEAREST TOWN
11 Blueberry Lake SRS	192	9	5	Valdez
12 Dry Creek SRS	320	58	4	Glennallen
13 Lake Louise SRA	90	20		Glennallen
14 Little Nelchina SRS	22	8		Glennallen
15 Little Tonsina SRS	102	8		Copper Center
16 Porcupine Creek SRS	240	12		Tok
17 Squirrel Creek SRS	325	14		Copper Center
18 Tolsona Creek SRS	600	11		Glennallen
19 Worthington Glacier SRS	113		3	Valdez

MAT-SU DISTRICT
P.O. Box 182
Palmer 99645

MAP KEY	ACREAGE	CAMP-SITES	PICNIC SITES	NEAREST TOWN
20 Big Lake (East) SRS	19	15	2	Wasilla
21 Big Lake (South) SRS	16	13	6	Wasilla
22 Bonnie Lake SRS	129	8		Palmer
23 Denali SP	421,120			Cantwell
Byers Lake		61	15	Cantwell
24 Finger Lake SRS	47	41		Palmer
25 Iditarod ST				
26 Independence Mine SHP	271			Palmer
27 Kepler Bradley SRA	111	undeveloped		Palmer
28 King Mountain SRS	20	22	2	Palmer
29 Long Lake SRS	480	8		Palmer
30 Matanuska Glacier SRS	229	12	5	Palmer
31 Moose Creek SRS	40	14	1	Palmer
32 Nancy Lake SRA	22,685			Willow
South Rolly Lake		106	20	Willow
33 Nancy Lake SRS	35	30	30	Willow
34 Rocky Lake SRS	48	10		Wasilla
35 Willow Creek SRS	240	17		Willow

CHUGACH DISTRICT
2601 Commercial Drive
Anchorage 99501

MAP KEY	ACREAGE	CAMP-SITES	PICNIC SITES	NEAREST TOWN
36 California Creek ST	58	undeveloped		Girdwood
37 Chugach SP	495,204			Anchorage
Bird Creek		25	14	Anchorage
Eagle River		36	12	Eagle River
Eklutna Lake		17	4	Eagle River
Upper Huffman			8	Anchorage
McHugh Creek			30	Anchorage
38 Mirror Lake SRS	90		30	Peters Creek
39 Peters Creek SRS	52	closed		Peters Creek
40 Thunderbird Falls ST	3			Eagle River

INTERIOR DISTRICT
4420 Airport Way
Fairbanks 99701

MAP KEY	ACREAGE	CAMP-SITES	PICNIC SITES	NEAREST TOWN
41 Chatanika River (lower) SRS	570	undeveloped		Fairbanks
42 Chatanika River (upper) SRS	73	15		Fairbanks
43 Chena River SRA	254,080	unlimited		Fairbanks
44 Chena River SRS	27		101	Fairbanks
45 Clearwater SRS	27	12		Delta Junction
46 Deadman Lake SRS	20	16		Tok
47 Donnelly Creek SRS	42	12		Delta Junction
48 Eagle Trail SRS	640	40	4	Tok
49 Gardiner Creek SRS	10	6		Tok
50 Harding Lake SRA	169	89	52	North Pole
51 Lakeview SRS	25	8		Tok
52 Moon Lake SRS	22	15		Tok
53 Quartz Lake SRS	380	13		Delta Junction
54 Rika's Landing SHS	10	undeveloped		Delta Junction
55 Salcha River SRS	61		20	North Pole
56 Tok River SRS	4	10		Tok

MAP KEY	ACREAGE	CAMP-SITES	PICNIC SITES	NEAREST TOWN
KENAI DISTRICT				
Box 1247				
Soldotna 99669				
57 Anchor River SRS	53	10		Homer
58 Anchor River SRA	208	409		Anchor Point
59 Bernice Lake SRS	152	17		Kenai
60 Bings Landing SRS	26	undeveloped		Sterling
61 Caines Head SRA	5,961	undeveloped		Seward
62 Captain Cook SRA	3,257			Kenai
Bishop Creek		12		Kenai
Discovery		57	30	Kenai
Stormy Lake		10	40	Kenai
Swanson River Canoe Landing				Kenai
63 Clam Gulch SRA	122	343	20	Soldotna
64 Deep Creek SRA	130	548	10	Ninilchik
65 Funny River SRS	202	3		Soldotna
66 Izaak Walton SRS	8	76		Soldotna
67 Johnson Lake SRA	325	46	24	Soldotna
68 Kachemak Bay SP	400,290	undeveloped		Homer
69 Kasilof River SRS	50	42	5	Kasilof
70 Kenai Keys SRA	193	undeveloped		Soldotna
71 Kenai River Island SRS	60	undeveloped		Soldotna
72 Kenai River (lower) SRS	20	undeveloped		Soldotna
73 Kenai River (upper) SRS	193	undeveloped		Sterling
74 Morgans Landing SRA	262		3	Sterling
75 Nilnunga SHP	42	undeveloped		Soldotna
76 Ninilchik SRA	97		137	Ninilchik
77 Slikok Creek SRS	40	undeveloped		Soldotna
78 Stariski SRS	30	13		Anchor Point
SOUTHWEST DISTRICT				
619 Warehouse Avenue, Suite 210				
Anchorage 99501				
79 Buskin River SRS	40	18		Kodiak
80 Fort Abercrombie SHP	183	14	15	Kodiak
81 Pasagshak River SRS	13			Kodiak
82 Wood-Tikchik SP	1,428,320	undeveloped		Dillingham

TIDES

In southeastern Alaska, Prince William Sound, Cook Inlet, and Bristol Bay, salt water undergoes extreme daily fluctuations, creating powerful tidal currents. Some bays may go totally dry at low tide. The second greatest tide range in North America occurs in upper Cook Inlet near Anchorage, where the maximum diurnal range during spring tides is 38.9 feet. (The greatest tide range in North America is Nova Scotia's Bay of Fundy with spring tides to 43 feet.)

Here are diurnal ranges for some coastal communities:

	FEET
Bethel	4.0
Cold Bay	7.1
Cordova	12.4
Haines	16.8
Herschel Island	0.7
Ketchikan	15.4
Kodiak	8.5
Naknek River entrance	22.6
Nikiski	20.7
Nome	1.6
Nushagak	19.6
Point Barrow	0.4
Port Heiden	12.3
Port Moller	10.8
Sand Point	7.3
Sitka	9.9
Valdez	12.0
Whittier	12.3
Wrangell	15.7
Yakutat	10.1

TIME ZONES

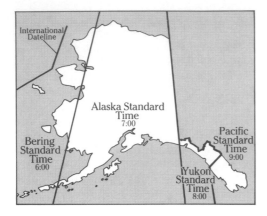

TOTEMS

In the early days of southeastern Alaska and British Columbia, the way of life of the Indian people living in these areas was based on the rich natural resources of the land, a respect for all living things, and a unique and complex social structure. The totemic art of the Indians is a reflection of this way of life. Totems are bold statements, making public records of the lives and history of the people who had them carved, and represent pride in clans and ancestors.

Totems, carved from yellow cedar, are a traditional art form among the Indians of British Columbia and southeastern Alaska. Although most well-known totems are tall and free standing, totemic art also was applied to houseposts and short entrance poles. The carved monuments were erected by the leading clans in each tribe in memory of their chiefs who had died. The poles also symbolized power and prestige.

Animals of the region are most often represented on the poles. Of all the crests, the frog appears most frequently, then the bear, eagle, raven, thunderbird, wolf, owl, grouse, starfish, finback whale, and halibut. Also represented are figures from Indian mythology: monsters with animal features, humanlike spirits, and semihistorical ancestors. Occasionally depicted are objects, devices, masks, and charms, and most rarely, art illustrating plants and sky phenomena.

The poles are traditionally painted with pigments made from coal, earth of yellow, brown, and red hues, cinnabar, berry juice, and spruce sap. Fungus found on hemlock produces various colors: yellow when decayed, red when roasted, and black when charred. Before modern paints became available, salmon eggs chewed with cedar bark formed the case, or glue, for the paint.

Totem art reached its peak after 1830, with the introduction of steel European tools acquired through fur trade. Leading families competed with others, building larger and more elaborate totem poles to show their wealth and prestige.

The pole was left to stand as long as nature would permit, usually no more than 50 to 60 years. Once a pole became so rotten that it fell, it was pushed aside, left to decay naturally or used for firewood. Most totem poles still standing in parks today are 40 to 50 years old. Heavy precipitation and acid muskeg soils hasten decomposition.

Collections of totem poles may be seen in several Alaska communities, including Ketchikan, Wrangell, and Sitka. Carvers may be seen practicing their art in Haines and Sitka.

A good source of more information is *Carved History, The Totem Poles and House Posts of Sitka National Historical Park*, published in cooperation with the National Park Service by the Alaska Natural History Association, Sitka Chapter, and is available from them for $2.65 postage-paid at P.O. Box 738, Sitka, Alaska 99835.

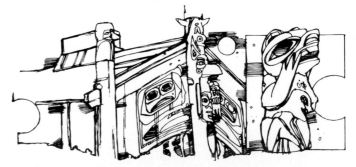

TRANS-ALASKA PIPELINE

The pipeline designer, builder, and operator is the Alyeska Pipeline Service Company, a consortium of the following eight oil companies:

Sohio Pipe Line Company	33.34%
ARCO Pipe Line Company	21.35%
Exxon Pipeline Company	20.34%
BP Pipelines Inc.	16.67%
Mobil Alaska Pipeline Company	4.08%
Union Alaska Pipeline Company	1.36%
Phillips Alaska Pipeline Corporation	1.36%
Amerada Hess Pipeline Corporation	1.50%

Pipeline length: 800 miles, slightly less than half that length is buried, the remainder is on 78,000 aboveground supports, located 60 feet apart, built in a flexible zigzag pattern. More than 800 river and stream crossings. Normal burial of pipe was used in stable soils and rock; aboveground pipe — insulated and jacketed — was used in permafrost areas. Thermal devices prevent thawing around vertical supports. 151 stop flow valves.

Pipe: Specially manufactured coated pipe with zinc anodes installed to prevent corrosion. Size is 48 inches in diameter, with thickness from 0.462 to 0.562 inch. Pipe sections before construction in lengths of 40 to 60 feet.

Cost: $8 billion, which includes terminal at Valdez, but does not include interest on money raised for construction.

Amount of oil pumped through pipeline: As of July 1981, 1.8 billion barrels of crude oil.

Operations: Control center at Valdez terminal and 10 operating pump stations along line monitor and control pipeline.

Pipeline capacity: By July 1981, 1.5 million barrels per day; can be increased to design

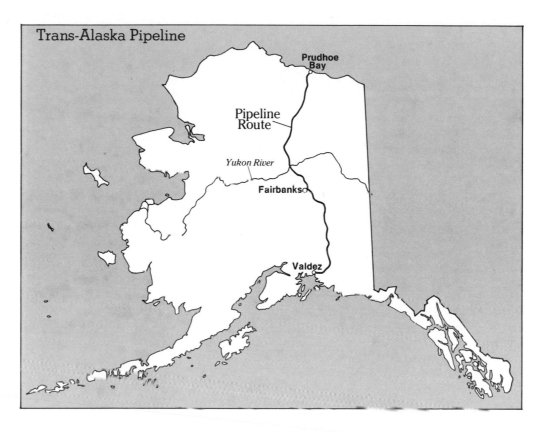

Trans-Alaska Pipeline

capacity of 2 million barrels per day by adding two pump stations and additional terminal facilities.

Estimated crude oil reserves recoverable on the North Slope: 9.4 billion barrels. Estimated hydrocarbon reserves: 26.5 trillion cubic feet.

Terminal: 1,000-acre site at Port Valdez, northernmost ice-free harbor in the U.S., with 18 tanks providing storage capacity of 9,180,000 barrels of oil.

Valdez ship-loading capacity: 110,000 barrels per hour for each of three berths; 80,000 barrels per hour for one berth.

Length and cost of pipeline haul road built by Alyeska: 360 miles, from the Yukon River to Prudhoe Bay, $150 million.

Yukon River bridge: First bridge (2,290 feet long) spanning the Yukon in Alaska.

Important dates: July, 1968, Prudhoe Bay oil field discovery confirmed; 1970, suits filed to halt construction, Alyeska Pipeline Service Company formed; November 16, 1973, presidential approval of pipeline legislation; April 29, 1974, construction begins on North Slope Haul Road (now the Dalton Highway) and is completed 154 days later; March 27, 1975, first pipe installed at Tonsina River; June 20, 1977, first oil leaves Prudhoe Bay, reaches Valdez terminal July 28; August 1, 1977, first tanker load of oil shipped aboard the SS *ARCO Juneau;* June 13, 1979, tanker number 1,000 (SS *ARCO Heritage*) sails.

UNIVERSITIES AND COLLEGES

Higher education in Alaska is provided by two private institutions and a statewide university system composed of three senior colleges, 10 community colleges and 11 rural education and extension centers.

The private colleges are Alaska Pacific University in Anchorage and Sheldon Jackson College in Sitka. Alaska Pacific is a four-year liberal arts college with a graduate program. Sheldon Jackson College began more than 100 years ago as a Presbyterian mission school for Tlingit Indians.

The three senior colleges in the statewide university system are located at Anchorage, Fairbanks, and Juneau. The 2,250-acre Fairbanks campus — research center for the statewide university system — is the state's largest campus and only residential campus. The 10 community colleges are degree-granting institutions. The rural education centers offer both credit and community service courses. Rural education centers are located at Adak, Cold Bay, Delta Junction, Dillingham, Fort Yukon, Galena, McGrath, Nenana, Sand Point, Tok, and Unalaska. For more information on rural education centers write the University of Alaska, Community Colleges, Rural Educational and Extension Affairs, 2221 E. Northern Lights Boulevard, Anchorage 99504. For information on colleges and universities, contact the following:

Alaska Pacific University
University Boulevard
Anchorage 99504

Anchorage Community College
2533 Providence Drive
Anchorage 99504

Kenai Peninsula
Community College
Box 848, Soldotna 99669

Ketchikan Community College
Box 358, Ketchikan 99901

Kodiak Community College
Box 946, Kodiak 99615

Kuskokwim Community College
Box 368, Bethel 99559

Matanuska-Susitna
Community College
Box 899, Palmer 99645

Northwest Community College
Box 400, Nome 99762

Prince William Sound
Community College
Box 590, Valdez 99686

Sheldon Jackson College
Box 479, Sitka 99835

Sitka Community College
Box 1090, Sitka 99835

Tanana Valley Community College
Constitution Hall
University of Alaska
Fairbanks 99701

University of Alaska, Anchorage
2651 Providence Drive
Anchorage 99504

University of Alaska, Fairbanks
Fairbanks 99701

University of Alaska, Juneau
11120 Glacier Highway
Juneau 99802

MISCELLANEOUS FACTS

State capital: Juneau.

Land area: 586,412 square miles or 375,296,000 acres — largest state in the union; one-fifth the size of the Lower 48.

Area per person: There are 1.5 square miles for each person in Alaska. New York has .003 square miles per person.

Diameter: East to west, 2,400 miles; north to south, 1,420 miles.

Coastline: 6,640 miles, point to point; as measured on the most detailed maps available, including islands, Alaska has 33,904 miles of shoreline. Estimated tidal shoreline, including islands, inlets and shoreline to head of tidewater is 47,300 miles.

Adjacent salt water: North Pacific Ocean, Bering Sea, Chukchi Sea, Arctic Ocean.

Alaska/Canada border: 1,538 miles long; Length of boundary between the Arctic Ocean and Mount Saint Elias is approximately 650 miles.

Geographic center: 63°50′ north, 152° west, about 60 miles northwest of Mount McKinley.

Northernmost point: Point Barrow, 71°23′ north.

Southernmost point: Tip of Amatignak Island, Aleutian Chain, 51°13′05″ north.

Easternmost and westernmost points: It all depends on how you look at it. The 180th meridian — halfway around the world from the prime meridian at Greenwich, England, and the dividing line between east and west longitudes — passes through Alaska. According to one view, therefore, Alaska has both the easternmost and westernmost spots in the country! The westernmost is Amatignak Island, 179°10′ west; and the easternmost is Pochnoi Point, 179°46′ east. On the other hand, if you are facing north, east is to your right and west to your left. Therefore, the westernmost point is Cape Wrangell, Attu Island, 172°27′ east; and the easternmost is in southeastern Alaska near Camp Point, 129°59′ west.

Farthest north supermarket: In Barrow; constructed on stilts to prevent snow build-up, at a cost of $4 million.

Tallest mountain: McKinley, 20,320 feet.

Largest natural freshwater lake: Iliamna, 1,000 square miles.

Longest river: Yukon, 1,400 miles in Alaska; 1,875 total.

Largest glacier: Malaspina, 850 square miles.

Largest city in population: Anchorage, population 174,431 (1980 U.S. census).

Largest city in area: Juneau with 3,108 square miles.

State motto: "North to the Future."

State flower: Forget-me-not, by an act of the territorial legislature April 28, 1917. The choice previously had been endorsed by the Grand Igloo of the Pioneers of Alaska.

State bird: Willow ptarmigan, declared the official bird of the territory February 4, 1955.

State tree: Sitka spruce, by an act of the 1962 state legislature.

State fish: King salmon, by an act of the state legislature, March 25, 1963.

State gem: Jade.

State mineral: Gold.

State sport: Dog mushing.

State flag: Big Dipper and North Star in gold on blue field.

State song: "Alaska's Flag."

Oldest building: Erskine House in Kodiak, built by the Russians, probably between 1793 and 1796.

191

Alaska Geographic. Back Issues

The Alaska Geographic Society

Box 4-EEE, Anchorage, AK 99509